Walking in your Anointing is your Investment in your Overflow!

Glenesha McIntosh

ISBN 979-8-9856703-6-3 (Paperback)

Copyright © 2025 by Glenesha McIntosh

All rights reserved. No part of this publication may be reproduced, distributed, or transmitted in any form or by any means-including photocopying, recording, or other electronic or mechanical methods for commercial purposes-without prior written permission of the Author. The only exception is brief quotations in printed reviews.

Author can be contacted via:
www.gmsunshinedevotionals.com

Churches may reproduce portions of this book without the express written permission of the Author, provided the text does not exceed 500 words or 5 percent of the entire book, whichever is less, and that the text is not material quoted from another publisher. When reproducing text from this book, include the following credit line:
"Walking in your Anointing is your Investment in your Overflow, written by Glenesha McIntosh, Used by permission."

Printed in the United States of America

Dear Reader,

I was graced with the opportunity to speak on a series of sermons at Hebron Evangelical Church (Brooklyn Campus), and the idea was suggested to me (by one of my bible school teachers, Minister Anthony Lovell), to put them into a book.

The truth is…

Many people have walked this road of Christianity for years, without ever stepping foot into the abundance and overflow of the life that Jesus came to give us (John 10:10). Many have given bountifully and sacrificially throughout the course of their lives, without having truly experienced what a pressed down, shaken together and running over life looks like (Luke 6:38). There is a table prepared before you in the presence of your enemies (Psalm 23:5), but how can you see or perceive what is prepared for you if you are not walking in your anointing? Walking in your anointing is what causes your cup to overflow. It is essentially your investment into your overflow.

As you read, you will unlock:
- The connection between prayer and your overflow

- Your vision, your steps, the light that takes precedence or the darkness that can hinder you - based on the substance of the source.
- The consistency that it takes to keep your flame burning.
- The cause and effect of being a two-edged sword [while understanding the cost as well as the damage that can be done if you cool off too quickly or resist being shaped into an effective tool].
- The Changes of everything and everyone around you, how to adapt, and press forward into your overflow.

I must say that…

It is truly a blessing to record the insight and illumination that God has given me into this book. Each message builds upon the next as the smoke that hurries out of a furnace as an indication of the presence of fire.

It is my hope that my dedication to the task, my studies and subsequently my presented teachings will be a blessing and an edification to you, as you pursue walking out your faith in a way that leads you directly into your anointing (a direct investment into your overflow), and a manifestation and full realization of living out an abundant life.

Be blessed,

G.M.

Foreword

Greeting in the name of Jesus.

My name is Anthony Lovell. I have been a member of Hebron Evangelical Church for many years.

I thank God for his Goodness and loving kindness, and for leading and guiding me by his Spirit.

Throughout my years of service, I was appointed a Deacon, then some years after that I was anointed as a Minister. I then became an Instructor at the Hebron Evangelical Bible School, and currently I am now the Associate Pastor of Hebron Evangelical Church (Brooklyn Campus).

As the Apostle Paul said, we as Christians must "study to shew thyself approved unto God, a workman that needeth not to be ashamed, rightly dividing the word of truth." 2 Timothy 2:15.
God rewards faithfulness! He will not withhold any good thing from those who walk uprightly (Ps 84:11).

To my sister in Christ, Glenesha…

I have known her for some time. She is a faithful member of the church at Hebron and has a zeal for God with good knowledge and understanding of the scriptures. I remember her coming to Bible school and in her 2nd year I had the privilege as one of her instructors in the word of God.

Now God is using her to preach and bring the message of salvation to others in these last and closing days.

I pray that God will continue to bless her with the spirit of wisdom and revelation as she inspires others to come closer to God in this dispensation of Grace.

Min. Anthony Lovell

The Prayer & The Overflow

Chapter I

The Prayer and the Overflow

INTRO:

Matthew 6:9-13

9 Our Father which art in heaven, Hallowed be thy name.

10 Thy kingdom come. Thy will be done in earth, as it is in heaven.

11 Give us this day our daily bread.

12 And forgive us our debts, as we forgive our debtors.

13 And lead us not into temptation, but deliver us from evil:

For thine is the kingdom, and the power, and the glory, for ever.

Amen.

I found it very interesting that in verse 12 of the Lord's prayer, most versions say forgive us our debts, or forgive us our sins, but I grew up hearing the version that says 'forgive us our trespasses'. And that is the version that many grew up saying but never know where the word 'trespasses' came from. Well, it came from the Matthew Bible version, which is now known as the New Matthew bible (NMB).

The Matthew's Bible was an early compilation of English translations of the books of the Bible and an important Bible of the English Reformation. It came into place back in 1537 by John Rogers under the name 'Thomas Matthew' and was considered the real primary version of our English Bible. It was a compilation of work from 3 men, including William Tyndale and Miles Coverdale who suffered greatly for their faith.

The Matthew's Bible was actually published 74 years before the KJV.

Just something interesting to note, that I came across in my studies 😊

MESSAGE:

My message is taken from both Matthew 6:9-13 KJV & Psalm 23:5-6 KJV

The Lord's Prayer is really a comprehensive prayer that covers everything.

Verse 9 says,

9 Our Father which art in heaven, Hallowed be thy name.

Although this prayer is a personal dialogue with God, I want you to see that even before we make a petition for ourselves - that we are making a declaration on behalf of everyone. We are acknowledging God, not specifically as the supreme being and creator of all, but more personally as the Father of everyone. Our Father, our Heavenly Father, may your name be kept Holy.

10 Thy kingdom come. Thy will be done in earth, as it is in heaven.

Here, we are welcoming the Lord's Holy Kingdom to be a home and covering for us, and we are requesting that God's WILL be done, both, in the physical as it is in the spiritual.

Is your physical life a manifestation of your Heavenly Father's will for you?

Although we hope for that life, how can we actually come into that realization?

We talked about versions of the bible, but what is God's version of you?

Do you think it looks anything like the version he created years ago (when he formed you in his perfect will)? Or does it look more like the way that the issues of life have shaped it to be?

If we mean this prayer, We are literally asking to reside in a kingdom (here on earth) where, because of the holiness of God, it requires a complete level of surrender [so that we look like, act like, walk like and talk like, the version of ourselves that God created us to be, in all creativity and uniqueness.]

If not,

We might as well stop the prayer right there, because we'll be walking down a road where there'll be stumbling blocks and barriers that will hinder the Father's daily bread for us. Because how can we live in a Holy Kingdom, where the Father's will is not done IN earth as it is in heaven. The Word literally becomes a double-edged sword, because if it is not wielded correctly it WILL lead to unfavorable outcomes.

It's a toss-up between eating based on the natural course and flow of life, or eating based on the favor and blessings that is in alignment with the will of God for an abundant life.

VERSE 11 says…

11 Give us this day our daily bread.

WHAT is the Lord saying to you daily and is there room for him to speak?

VERSE 12 says…

12 And forgive us our debts, as we forgive our debtors.

THIS IS A BIG ONE.

Many versions speak of this scripture as a past tense, rather than a present;

They say, as we have 'forgiven' our debtors, whereas the King James says, as we forgive (in a more present tense). But whether past or present, we make mistakes all the time that end up costing us dearly. And at those times we find ourselves at the feet of the Lord asking for him to wipe our slate clean or give us a fresh start.

At such times, we have nothing to give in return and nothing to bargain with. But Jesus is our mediator ready to plead our case, in accordance with the conditions associated with our request.

The scripture says 'as we forgive our debtors'.

What did you do the last time someone stepped on your toes (literally or figuratively)?

What do you hold in your heart against the person that stole the credit for your work?

We are asking for the Lord to allow us to be treated the same way that we treat others [REGARDLESS of whose in the wrong or right.]

We are asking for him to release us from our obligations, the same way we have released others from their obligations to us [Regardless of who owes who.]

We are asking for us to be forgiven from our actions the way we've forgiven others from their actions [Regardless or whom did what to whom.]

Again, it is a 2-edged sword, that can either work in our favor or not, based on our past and present actions.

Verse 13 says,

13 And lead us not into temptation, but deliver us from evil:

Have you ever wondered why this scripture will be leading us in a prayer that asks the Lord not to lead us into temptation, but deliver us from evil?

James 1:13-15 NIV says "When tempted, no one should say, "God is tempting me." For God cannot be tempted by evil, nor does he tempt anyone; 14 but each person is tempted when they are dragged away by their own evil desire and enticed. 15 Then, after desire has conceived, it gives birth to sin; and sin, when it is full-grown, gives birth to death."

Then Psalm 141:4 NIV says "Do not let my heart be drawn to what is evil so that I take part in wicked deeds along with those who are evildoers; do not let me eat their delicacies."

So what does Matthew 12:13 really mean when it says 'lead us not into temptation'?

In the prayer, what we are really asking our heavenly Father, is to not leave us - but to protect us.

Isn't it typical that after we have sinned or done wrong, and have reached the point to humble ourselves and ask for forgiveness – Isn't it human nature to think…

- Will what we've done, or how we've acted, or what we've said, push others away?

If someone doesn't care, and everything that happens - they're just quick to put it behind them [with no resolution and no sincere apologies; just a nonchalant attitude about everything], then the Lord's prayer is not for them.

But after we've just asked for forgiveness and asked the Lord to handle us in the way we've handled others (because that's what we deserve); [If the Lord's response causes a strain in our relationship with the him, and his presence was to be removed from us (from our hearts), or maybe the distance in our relationship with him widens] - then our hearts (which the bible says is deceitful above all things), will naturally be drawn into temptation to the things of this world and what looks delectable to it.

So we're saying to the Lord is, don't step away from us - because just your presence delivers us from our hearts desiring evil.

What we desire is the table that the Lord has prepared for us. That trumps any kind of temptation that the world can offer us.

In Psalm 23 NIV, Verse 5 says

5 You prepare a table before me in the presence of my enemies.

In this context, enemies doesn't mean people who hate you. When we are not lead down the road of temptation, but are delivered from evil, your enemies are not who you think they are. They can simply be people who are not aligned with the will of God and therefore not designated to eat with you at your table at such given time or season.

For example, when Jesus said to Peter in *Matthew 16:23 NIV "Get behind me, Satan! You are a stumbling block to me; you do not have in mind the concerns of God, but merely human concerns."* But at the same time Peter is also, the same one who Jesus said, in Matthew 16:18 KJV (just a few verses before) *"upon this rock I will build my church; and the gates of hell shall not prevail against it."*

Your enemies are not going to look like the rest of the world's enemies. Sometimes they'll look like the ones closest to you.

Jesus calling Peter Satan, did not mean that he considered Peter to be the evil one. But at that time and season in Jesus' walk, Peter easily became an offense to Jesus, as he was not aligned to his purpose.

Many times, people can be privy to your purpose and can listen to the will of God but not be hearers. Meaning one who receives with a level of understanding from God and surrenders to the cause.

BUT even hearers can accept God's will for your lives, in as much as they will not intentionally interfere or interrupt with what the Lord is doing, BUT they can remain without ACTION, attempting to satisfy human emotions by lack of involvement, and even resort to simply pacifying religious rituals that God is trying to step out of and do a new thing - and THEREBY they can still indirectly become a hinderance to your calling.

Hearers can be anyone.

Did you know that the Lord has the power to open up one's understanding so that people can have a conviction only for a set time and season, so that will of God can come to pass?

Have you ever seen someone who was against you or constantly trying to trip you up, actually vouch for you in a time that it really mattered? Did it strike you with astonishment?

What about people that you thought would judge you harshly and look down on you, but when you had no choice but to go to them and ask for their help, you were amazed at how they were so understanding and moved to make things happen - just for you. And they don't even know God the way you do.

Such conviction can be done, simply by God's divine power cancelling out the effects of the enemy (which is the temptation, the distraction and the noise) for a selected period of time, so that your road will not be hindered.

As a disciple we are called to be more than hearers. We have greater responsibility.

James 1:22 KJV says *"But be ye doers of the word, and not hearers only, deceiving your own selves."*

The bible also says that if we resist the devil he will flee. Which means that we shouldn't abuse the divine power of God. Our trained willpower has to kick in, because he lives in us. So, we have to exercise our God-given authority to be a hearer and doer of the word.

Psalm 23 Verse 5 continues to say,

"You anoint my head with oil; my cup overflows."

As a child in Kingdom of God, being anointed is your portion. But without faith, you are stifling your investment in your overflow.

Walking in your anointing is your investment in your overflow, and it can only come through faith; because we walk by faith and not by sight (2 Cor. 5:7).

Matthew 21:22 says that if you have faith, you will receive what you ask in prayer.

The issue then becomes, are you lacking the kind of faith necessary to walk in your anointing that facilitates your investment in your overflow.

....

There are 2 kinds of faith.

There is Faith (the belief) and Faith (the gift)

Faith (the belief): By definition, means to completely have trust or confidence in someone or something. And although it is generally understood by many as a word that indicates having a strong belief in God, this belief can only define your reverence in the known character of what/who you are having faith in.

For example, you don't need to have the gift of faith to believe that the elevator chains are not going to snap as it carries you up to the 30th floor, you just need faith – the belief. This is not the same faith that gives you the confident assurance in what God WILL DO.

Many people operate on this false expectation and live their lives under the notion of a mere hope that God WILL, just because they love him and treat others good. But they don't realize that they are not lining up with the faith that is required to reveal to them the actual truth.

John 16:13 ESV says *"When the Spirit of truth comes, he will guide you into all the truth, for he will not speak on his own authority, but whatever he hears he will speak, and he will declare to you the things that are to come."*

Because the Holy Spirit is a personal relationship, you cannot solely depend on Pastors or leaders to declare to you the things that are to come. **The Holy Spirit, which is the Spirit of Truth, has to be speaking to you from within. This is your daily bread.**

Faith (the gift): Occurs through a process.

Romans 10:17 says that faith comes from hearing and hearing through the word of God. Meaning, that we hear what the Lord is saying TO US through the Holy Spirit's revelation, illumination, and direction through the Word of God.

People can say they have faith (the belief) – but really, they have a false expectation of a **possible** favorable response from God while living life based on their own learned knowledge, feeling, and direction, rather than by the Gift of Faith, that tells you, shows you (through visions or dreams), or downloads to you (to the point where you can feel it), the things that are to come.

People go to church for years, and still cannot discern the voice of God, because the gift of faith have not been matured and exercised. And that's not something you should feel bad about, that's something that you should seek after.

There is a level of responsibility you ought to have over your own faith walk that makes you a recipient of the anointing in the Kingdom of God that leads to your overflow.

There's a reason people go through rehabilitation, after a situation that puts them in a space where they need to improve their mobility needed for their daily life. But sadly, some people use rehab, that is meant to help them become more independent, to create a lifelong dependency.

The Lord is saying, when it comes to situations that help you to grow, don't confuse the season, as a lifelong attachment.

The Holy Spirit, the Spirit of Truth is seeking an interdependent relationship with you, where together, you can live in the abundant life he has for you.

Stop settling for just enough!

Stop being satisfied with just ok!

That kind of thinking is what put Peter in that predicament to become an offense to the Lord.

I can guarantee you that God's will for you is not to remain stagnant, or to remain where you are right now.

When older people are passionate for God, it drives them insane when they look at the younger folks who are not doing anything with their youthful benefits.

And when the younger people are on fire for God, it actually drives them out of the church, when they look at older folks who don't give them the permission and support to spread their wings.

How can the lost know that God is bigger, if everything they accomplish in the world is bigger than what the children of God is accomplishing?

How can they desire the things of God, if our lives don't reflect that abundant life that God has for us?

Do not pass up your anointing and your overflow!

Exercise and GROW your gift of faith. The spirit of truth is waiting for you to hear him, because he's constantly speaking.

In Closing,,

Psalm 23:6 says…

"Surely goodness and mercy shall follow me all the days of my life: and I will dwell in the house of the LORD for ever."

This ties us back into the Lord's Prayer in Matthew 6:13.

"For thine is the kingdom, and the power, and the glory, for ever. Amen."

Chapter 1 - Author's remarks

In this sermon, the Lord revealed some very important things to me.

Prayer is more than our verbal conversation with God. It is the very motion of our lives.

The Lord's prayer literally shows us a blueprint to a successful life of overflow:

It teaches us –

1. the way we should honor God,

2. the way we ought to honor his house,

3. the daily direction we need to receive from him,

4. the importance of the way we treat others,

5. how imperative it is to stay in his presence (so that we are not left to the mercies of temptation)

… and it essentially teaches us

6. how the process of our faith walk leads us into our anointing that is substantiated by his goodness, mercy, favor and faithfulness [which produces the overflow of life's abundance and thereby demonstrates the Kingdom, power, and glory that dwells in the house of the Lord – for ever. Amen.]

The Shadow & The Substance

Chapter 2

The Shadow and the Substance

RECAP:

The last message was about the Lord's prayer and a full acknowledgement of what we are really praying for, which requires a complete level of surrender that brings out the version of ourselves that God created us to be in all of our creativity and uniqueness.

I spoke about how our surrender is vital in receiving our daily bread, which is the Holy Spirit [the Spirit of Truth] speaking to us from within.

The scripture says that he anoints your head with oil and your cup overflows. In other words - walking in your anointing is your investment in your overflow, and it can only come through faith, because we walk by faith and not by sight.

Without faith, you are stifling your investment to your overflow!

I spoke about the difference between Faith (the belief) and Faith (the gift). Faith the belief means to completely have trust or confidence in someone or something, but that kind of faith comes with a false expectation that God WILL, just because of ones love for him and being a good person [doing the right thing].

But Faith the gift occurs through a process of hearing what the Lord is saying to us through revelation, illumination, and an understanding that directs us through the Word of God.

It's the difference between a possible favorable response while living a life based on one's own learned knowledge, feeling and direction, rather than by the Gift of Faith, that tells you, shows you (through visions, dreams, or downloads, the things that are to come and the way in which you should go.

Maturing/growing the gift of Faith is necessary to exercise your faith walk; and that is what makes you a recipient of the anointing in the Kingdom of God that leads to your overflow.

This is what creates the umph, zeal, and ambition to continue to press forward no matter the circumstance.

INTRO:

In 2 Corinthians 6:3-13 Paul speaks of many hardships that we endure; expressing that despite it all, if our hearts are open to others (without a lack of love), we would live in such a way that no one will stumble because of us, and no one will blame the ministry either. Because in everything that we do, we show that we are true people of God who demonstrate a lot of patience despite our troubles, our labors, our sleeplessness, and so on.

We show kindness!

And where others give a bad report, we counter with a good report. No matter the sorrows, or who is crying trouble, we will rejoice. If poor - we give plentifully out of the riches of our hearts; and even if we have nothing, we still possess everything.

This way of life is a level of contentment that Paul speaks about in Philippians 4:12, that does not contradict your increase into your overflow by posing as what many think contentment is, which is being comfortable.

Contentment is not comfortability!

Being comfortable has a way of keeping you stagnant and causing you to simply remain where you are, because there is an ease and freedom of stress. In fact, being comfortable is one way to gauge whether you're living a self-guided life, or a purpose-driven life through Christ.

I heard the Lord say to me, that stress is not what people make it out to be, but that it was actually meant to:

S - tretch your capacity, and cause you to

T - hink under pressure. It makes you exercise

R – estraint. It teaches you how to

E – ndure. It

S - hows you what you're capable of, and it builds your

S - trength.

Stress is indeed a significant contributor to many health problems. But that is only because we have not been properly trained to identify it and use it correctly, therefore it destroys us.

Hosea 4:6 says *"My people are destroyed for lack of knowledge"*.

This is not a woke statement!

I know that we are in this error of awakening. In Hosea chapter 4 the Lord is actually bringing charge against the people of the land for their lack of faithfulness, kindness and knowledge of him.

While the Lord is deeply offended by their behavior, he makes a statement using the word **'my'** which is a possessive adjective.

Possessive adjective's modifies a noun to show ownership or possession.

*"**MY** people perish because of lack of knowledge".*

The knowledge He is referring to is the knowledge of God!

<u>In the old testament, the knowledge of God was carried out through obedience to His law.</u>

In this day and age, or in this dispensation of Grace, the Law was fulfilled through the life of Jesus Christ, which now flows through the Holy Spirit that resides in us, leading us into all truth, which is the knowledge of God, which is His perfect Will.

If we lack direction through His Will, we basically perish at the mercies of this world, because we are essentially lacking in the knowledge of the Lord.

It's the difference between walking in your shadow or walking in substance.

MESSAGE:

The bible says resist the devil and he will flee. But what do you do about the thing you can't flee from? Your shadow.

My daughter has a show that she watches from time to time. In one episode, two children are playing a game of catch and a little toddler named George, is in the middle [but he's not trying to catch the ball; he's trying to catch its shadow].

As the ball is thrown between the two children. The children explain to George that the shadow is not the ball, but that it is actually its shadow.

George watches as he observes the ball's shadow. Then the children show George that he also has a shadow. He then tries to walk away from his shadow. The children giggle and tell him that he can't walk away from his shadow, but that he has to run away from it.

They demonstrate, and then realize that that didn't work.

Another friend comes along on a scooter and sees what they're doing, and she says, you can't run away from your shadow, you have to ride away from it.

She then demonstrates and also realizes that that didn't work either.

A dad and his two children come along and the other children tell him that they're all trying to run away from their shadow. So the dad says, you can't run away from your shadow; and then he demonstrates that no matter how fast you run, you can't run away from your shadow. He explains that your shadow always stays with you. Then the dad's little toddler son, (whom I guess is obviously knowledgeable about shadows), tells the children, that 'when something gets in the way of the sun, it makes a shadow'. Then his dad boasts that he has the biggest shadow because he is the biggest; and then his toddler son, stated that him and George (the other toddler) has the smallest shadows, because they are the smallest.

Then something interesting happened. They all looked at their shadows and noticed that their shadows were getting longer. The dad explains that that's because the sun is setting because it is nearly nighttime.

The children noticed that their shadows eventually went away and the dad explained lastly, that it's because the sun has set.

A shadow represents a partial area of darkness or obscurity that is caused by a body intercepting the light; and the shadow is always cast in the opposite direction of the sun.

So if that body is walking away from the source of light, their shadow will always seem to go forward ahead of them.

In the Greek, the word 'shadow' is called skia, and it has a 2 part reference. a. It is a shade that is 'caused by the interception of light' and b. it is an image or outline cast by an object. Both the words shadow and shade are used interchangeably throughout the bible. And like most things, it can be wielded as a two edged sword.

Substance on the other hand, has a 4 part meaning.

1. It is described as the essential nature or the essence of something or someone [their quality and characteristics].

2. It is also described as the ultimate reality that is the basis of all outward manifestations [including all usefulness and importance].

3. Substance is also described as the full makeup of something or someone (it's composition or structure), and the act of combining all the parts to form a whole [including the fundamental laws or the basic principles that make it an interconnecting network that affects temperament and health, as well as outcomes].

4. Substance is also described as possessions.

Psalm 24:1-2 NIV says that *"The earth is the Lord's, and everything in it, the world, and all who live in it; for he founded it on the seas and established it on the waters."*

I want to speak about these 2 edges of the sword:

- The shadow/shade that is the image or outline cast by you or others [representing a self-led life that only occurs when something gets in the way of the **son**].

&

- The shadow/shade that is cast by a God himself [the substance] or spoken of as a representation of a place for us to take refuge, or a covering, or a symbol or copy of something. It also represents a warning or indication of something to come, a present reality or a time-frame, or a sign from the Lord.

I'll be breaking it down further into 4 sections, while referencing God as the substance and the source of the light – both as the sun (S-U-N) and Jesus the son (S-O-N).

1. The shadow cast by you

2. The shadow cast by others

3. The shadow cast by God

4. And the Shadow/shade spoken of as a representation

1. The Shadow cast by you

What does it mean when we cast a shadow?

When we cast a shadow, if the sun is at it's peak – overhead, we block the light source of the immediate surrounding area that we're standing in. And if the sun is rising or setting, the lengthening image of our shadow can be seen cast in the opposite direction of the sun, no matter which direction we're facing. *Not that you don't know this…*

If you think about it, we don't logically and physically just walk in darkness without any form of light. And on the other hand, it's hard to see where we're going, if we're walking directly into the beaming sunlight, without some time of shades on. So having shade does serve a purpose!

The reality is, as long as the source of light, lights up everything around us, it gives us perspective so that we can naturally walk by sight. It's built into our instinctive makeup, and that's where so many of our emotions comes in [because we focus on what we see and we react based on our feelings].

The problem is that we focus-in so much on one thought, that it materializes into our decision making and leads us into what we say and do.

If we were to take away that light, we wouldn't have perspective; because there wouldn't be a point of view to base our emotions or feelings on [to have a particular attitude toward something]. So when you think about it, it's really hard to lead your own life naturally, without having light!

But with that light, the reality is that we go through life walking in our own shadow, because the light flows around our image making us self-centered individuals [whether or not we are aware that God is the substance and that he is always watching].

But when the substance, who is God, comes into our hearts and renews our minds, it changes the direction of our perspective.

Now instead of walking by sight, we walk by faith!

Suddenly, when we see things [before our emotions or our feelings kicks in], discernment precedes it. Discernment guides our ability to judge what emotions are effective to us, on account of what's before us.

But it goes further than just what is seen, it also guides us in preparation for what is unseen.

It presents choices before us to preset a particular spiritual attitude, that paves the way to allow us to hear what the Lord is saying through spiritual guidance.

This is where Psalm 23:4 NKJV comes in, that says *"Yea, though I walk through the valley of the shadow of death, I will fear no evil; For You are with me; Your rod and Your staff, they comfort me."* **Meaning that even though we are walking through life with a predisposed shadow of Self. Through faith, the substance of God walks with us, and that in itself is the spiritual death of ignorance.**

2. The Shadow cast by others

Many have heard the phrase 'throwing shade'. It is basically to criticize someone or something, and show that you don't respect them. It's the practice of reading subtle, indirect critiques and interpreting them as direct insults.

It's the idea that someone thinks so little of you, that they'll throw their most poorly thought of image, upon you.

The damage that others can do to your thoughts about yourself, is quite significant, if you believe them.

The damage that others can do to your character, can also be quite significant, if hearers believe them.

Will you walk in a tainted shadow?

To walk in a tainted shadow is to cancel out both your instinctive nature of the self-led walking by sight as well as the renewed nature of the spirit-led walking by faith, and to walk in the shadow of someone that you don't recognize altogether.

Have you ever been there?

Have you ever been to the place where you couldn't recognize yourself or didn't even know who you were anymore? All because there was so much noise and so many people speaking into you and about you, and you can barely hear what God is saying [if at all].

Now, what if the shadow cast by others doesn't necessarily seem or look bad?

What about if others saw something in you, or saw you as something completely different than what you had your eyes set on or where you thought God was trying to lead you? What if they made you out to be something that you're just, not.

They constantly pitch a speech that you're something bigger, better, or just different than who you are.

It can seem forceful, or thrown on you. It can seem like they're trying to shape you or change you, or even create a better or bigger you. Or maybe it just seems a bit much. Like if they're trying to 'gas you up'. They're constantly complimenting, praising, or excessively attempting to inflate your ego or give you a boost of confidence (public displays of dramatic flattery).

Maybe there's some hidden suggestions in there, or indirect hints of some things are indeed things that needs to be changed or brought to your attention or at least considered. Or maybe it's all a load of crap!

How do you respond? Is there any truth to it?

Is their intention to make you walk puffed up, just so that others will aim to humble you. Or are they really genuinely in awww of you?

We all experience some form or the other.

Some of these experiences can come from family, friends, or acquaintances; but some are your enemies.

How do you tell whose who?

Are their comments just out of nowhere, or does it fit the occasion as genuine truth?

When you come before the Lord, what do you ask for, for your enemies?

Your enemies that have walked on you and trampled your name, or snatch away your opportunities, or looked upon you with disgust?

When your prayer sounds like *Psalm 109:21-23 NIV "Sovereign Lord, help me for your name's sake; out of the goodness of your love, deliver me. For I am poor and needy, and my heart is wounded within me. I fade away like an evening shadow;"*

Psalm 109 is called an imprecatory psalm, meaning that it calls down a curse. Although I read you the 'poor is me verses', if you read the whole chapter, it is quite intense with calling down judgement for ones enemies.

One of the things I've learned is that although Psalms like these can make people wonder, how can we love our enemies yet call down thunder and lighting for them. In actuality, these types of psalms do not have personal ill feelings for their enemies, as it is not based off of human grudges, but rather divine justice. This imprecatory prayer in Psalm 109 committed the enemies to the justice of God for their due reward.

I would presume that to get to this place, one would have most likely suffered long and were constantly rewarded evil for good and hatred for love. It usually leaves the one going through the anguish with two choices of prayers. Either you pray that God has mercy when the justice of God strikes, or you commit them to the justice of God.

Usually, people ask God to have mercy on those who don't really know what they're doing [the ones who are just blinded by the lies of the enemy without full and proper understanding].

When dealing with our enemies, if we receive spiritual guidance from the substance, who is God; we will ensure that even as we walk in our shadow (that has the ability to be self-seeking and self-advocating), that we subdue self-led thinking so that we don't get entangled in our enemies judgement by mishandling the situation.

1 Corinthians 9:27 NLT says *"I discipline my body like an athlete, training it to do what it should. Otherwise, I fear*

that after preaching to others I myself might be disqualified."

3. The Shadow cast by God

In 2 Kings 20:1-11 NIV King Hezekiah was sick unto death due to a deadly boil. The scripture says, *"The prophet Isaiah son of Amoz went to him and said, "This is what the Lord says: Put your house in order, because you are going to die; you will not recover." 2 Hezekiah turned his face to the wall and prayed to the Lord, 3 "Remember, Lord, how I have walked before you faithfully and with wholehearted devotion and have done what is good in your eyes." And Hezekiah wept bitterly. 4 Before Isaiah had left the middle court, the word of the Lord came to him: 5 "Go back and tell Hezekiah, the ruler of my people, 'This is what the Lord, the God of your father David, says: I have heard your prayer and seen your tears; I will heal you. On the third day from now you will go up to the temple of the Lord. 6 I will add fifteen years to your life. And I will deliver you and this city from the hand of the king of Assyria. I will defend this city for my sake and for the sake of my servant David.' " 7 Then Isaiah said, "Prepare a poultice of figs."* (which is a traditional medical remedy made by mashing fresh or dried figs and applying them to the skin) *They did so and applied it to the boil, and he recovered."*

Now him recovering doesn't mean that he was healed. Recovery means that he was able to return to a prior level of function/performance. Remember that Hezekiah was sick unto death. But to take hold of God's promise and have all these years added to his life, he had to go up to the temple of the Lord. So there had to be some level of recovery for him to do that; and Hezekiah was well aware that human remedy is not enough to heal him and give him this increase.

Verse 8-9 says "Hezekiah had asked Isaiah, *"What will be the sign that the Lord will heal me and that I will go up to the temple of the Lord on the third day from now?" 9 Isaiah answered, "This is the Lord's sign to you that the Lord will do what he has promised: Shall the shadow go forward ten steps, or shall it go back ten steps?"*

Isn't it amazing that God made a promise to Hezekiah, and still included him in the process by giving him a choice, of how he wanted the sign to be displayed. Shall the shadow go forward ten steps, or shall it go back ten steps?"

Verse 10-11 says, *"It is a simple matter for the shadow to go forward ten steps," said Hezekiah. "Rather, have it go back ten steps." 11 Then the prophet Isaiah called on the Lord, and the Lord made the shadow go back the ten steps it had gone down on the stairway of Ahaz."*

The stairway of Ahaz was believed to have been some form of a sundial or timekeeping device. Maybe like a stone age clock. So the sign that the Lord gave Hezekiah was one that appeared to move the time by 10 steps. But Hezekiah chose for the shadow to instead go back 10 steps.

Hezekiah appeared to have been given a symbolic opportunity to either reclaim time that was lost or move forward into his next season; and he made a bold choice and a statement [in confirmation of God's promise], by seeing the shadow go back 10 steps as a sign of God's healing and also a sign for him to go up to the temple for his increase.

In the face of a negative report or a trying circumstance, have you ever had to remind God of your faithfulness and wholehearted devotion?

Have your weeping ever caused your fate to change?

Have God revealed to you any promises?

Have you asked God for a sign?

Here's an important question. Because many people are very skeptical about receiving treatment for their issues, while they pray and pray for God to heal them.

Are you willing to accept the human remedy that has been put together for you, as your form of recovery, while you wait on your healing from the Lord and your increase?

4. The Shadow/shade spoken of as a representation:

The Shadow spoken of as a representation signifies, through various scriptures, an indication of the present reality or something to come, a covering, a refuge or shelter, or a time-frame.

These are just a few…

The Shadow: *Colossians 2:16-17 AMP - "Therefore let no one judge you in regard to food and drink or in regard to [the observance of] a festival or a new moon or a Sabbath day. 17 Such things are only a shadow of what is to come and they have only symbolic value; but the substance [the reality of what is foreshadowed] belongs to Christ."*

The Shade: *Mark 4:30-32 NKJV - "To what shall we liken the kingdom of God? Or with what parable shall we picture it? 31 It is like a mustard seed which, when it is sown on the ground, is smaller than all the seeds on earth; 32 but when it is sown, it grows up and becomes greater than all herbs, and shoots out large branches, so that the birds of the air may nest under its shade."*

The shadow and the shade speaks of an indication of something to come and the present reality.

The Shadow: *Psalm 36:7 KJV - "How excellent is thy lovingkindness, O God! therefore the children of men put their trust under the shadow of thy wings."*

The Shade: *Jonah 4:6 NIV - "Then the LORD God provided a leafy plant and made it grow up over Jonah to give shade for his head to ease his discomfort, and Jonah was very happy about the plant."*

The shadow and the shade speaks of covering.

The Shadow: *Hosea 14:7 NKJV - "Those who dwell under his shadow shall return; They shall be revived like grain, And grow like a vine. Their scent shall be like the wine of Lebanon."*

The Shade: *Psalm 121:5 NKJV - "The LORD is your keeper; The LORD is your shade at your right hand."*

The shadow and the shade speaks of refuge and shelter.

The Shadow: *1 Chronicles 29:15 KJV - "For we are strangers before thee, and sojourners, as were all our fathers: our days on the earth are as a shadow, and there is none abiding."*

The Shade: *Job 7:1-2 NKJV - "Is there not a time of hard service for man on earth? Are not his days also like the days of a hired man? Like a servant who earnestly desires the shade, And like a hired man who eagerly looks for his wages,"*

The shadow and the shade speaks of a time-frame.

…..

In Closing,

When something gets in the way of the sun, it makes a shadow. And as long as there is light, we will always have a shadow. But we have a daily task to choose whether to be self-led or spirit led.

Psalm 91:1 AMP says *"He who dwells in the shelter of the Most High Will remain secure and rest in the shadow of the Almighty [whose power no enemy can withstand]."*

With the substance, who is God, our natural vision is filtered through our spiritual vision that brings a confident assurance in what we hope for.

This hope reestablishes our shadow (what used to be our self-led life) with a spirit-led life [giving us a revelation of the present reality and things to come, a covering, a refuge, a shelter, and a time-frame].

Therefore wherever we go - he is there, whatever we eat - he blesses, whatever we offer to him – he multiplies, and whenever we rest – he restores. Amen.

Chapter 2 - Author's remarks

I received so much understanding and insight in regard to how the Lord is literally transforming the lives of his people. He is showing us who we are, who we've been, and who we are going to be. He is reteaching and flipping the script [on what we used to think was our crippling limitations], and he is unveiling the truth behind the masks.

He is, has always been and will always be the timekeeper, the time giver, and the time taker.

We only receive the effectual operation of his shade and his shadow [that covers and protects, guides and provides, and warns and foreshadows], if we accept the renewed nature of spirit-led walking by faith through a daily acknowledgement and surrender to the substance.

Ecclesiastes 9:11 NLT says, *"I have observed something else under the sun. The fastest runner doesn't always win the race, and the strongest warrior doesn't always win the battle. The wise sometimes go hungry, and the skillful are not necessarily wealthy. And those who are educated don't always lead successful lives. It is all decided by chance, by being in the right place at the right time."*

Chance is 'the possibility of'.

Because we don't know the future, all we have as self-led individuals [walking in our own shadows] is 'the possibility of'.

King Solomon tested out many theories about life, but the one thing he could not experience was the Holy Spirit living on the inside of him.

In this dispensation of Grace, the Holy Spirit that dwells on the inside of us, gives us a renewed vision that changes our possibilities into confirmations [providing a substance and a surety of what is yet to come], and ALWAYS places us in the right place - at the right time [ensuring the certainty of the Lord's promises for you].

It opens the right doors and closes the wrong ones. It speeds up what we need now [for our present reality] and it delays what we are not yet lined up for. It stores up and it releases, ensuring that no matter the odds lined up against us, that we always WIN.

Consistency fans the Flame

Chapter 3

Consistency Fans the Flame

RECAP:

In my first message, I spoke about prayer and how our surrender is vital in receiving our daily bread, and that walking in your anointing is your investment in your overflow. This can only come through faith - that is more than confidence, it is actually the evidence of the process of revelation, illumination, and an understanding, that directs us through the Word of God - into the things that are to come.

I spoke about how contentment is not comfortability. Being comfortable has a way of keeping you stagnant (causing you to simply remain where you are), because there is an ease and a freedom from stress. Being comfortable is one way to gauge whether you're living a self-guided life, or a purpose-driven life through Christ.

I spoke of a redefining of STRESS.

That it **S**tretches your capacity, causes you to **T**hink under pressure, exercise **R**estraint; it teaches **E**ndurance, it **S**hows you what you're capable of, and it builds your **S**trength.

Stress is only a significant contributor to many health problems because we have not been properly trained to identify and use it correctly, therefore it destroys us. Proverbs 17:3 says that the furnace is for gold, and Genesis 2:12 says that the gold of that land is good.

A significant portion of the earth's gold is found in the ground, in deposits. It is scooped out of the land and put through a method called sluicing (where miners use water to wash the dirt in order to separate the gold). Gold, which is heavier than dirt is then sifted and trapped by obstacles through a process, while the other gravel/sand/dirt are washed away by the current.

The process that gold has to go through in order to be purified or refined, is not just melting it down and reforming it again. It includes multiple steps such as crushing, grinding, melting, thickening, oxidation, chlorination, and a lot of boiling at really high temperatures. The interesting thing is that the gold always sinks to the bottom. It's weighty, it's heavy but it is highly valued.

People don't want gold in its raw form, they want it in its purified/refined form. They want it to be shaped and be beautiful and eye catching. No one even thinks about the number of tests that have to be done and samples that have to be taken, to ensure that the process is actually separating what is pure from the other metals that have been attached to it for so long.

In Luke 22:31-32 AMP the Lord said, *"Simon, Simon (Peter), listen! Satan has demanded permission to sift [all of] you like grain; 32 but I have prayed [especially] for you [Peter], that your faith [and confidence in Me] may not fail;"*

As much as Jesus loved Peter, he did not say that he has taken him out of the sifting process. He said that he prayed for him. Meaning you have to go through the process, in order for your life to be redefined.

Satan thinks that he is doing you an injustice [but believe it or not], even his works are an instrumental part of the process.

In my second message, I spoke about the shadow and the substance.

When something gets in the way of the sun, it makes a shadow.

Our shadow (that has the ability to be self-seeking and self-advocating). It reveals perspective, which engages our humanity to walk by sight. Eve walked by sight. Satan presented to her a point of view, which connected with her emotions to prioritize her instinctive nature.

She did as any human or child would do, who is not fully surrendered to the Lord.

But the substance of God puts to death spiritual ignorance [by a renewal of our mind that changes the direction of our perspective] by introducing discernment to guide our emotions in preparation for what is seen and unseen. It presents choices before us to preset a particular spiritual attitude, that paves the way to allow us to hear what the Lord is saying through spiritual guidance so that we walk by faith.

Psalm 23:4 NKJV says *"Yea, though I walk through the valley of the shadow of death, I will fear no evil; For You are with me; Your rod and Your staff, they comfort me."*

Meaning even though we are walking through life with a predisposed shadow of Self; through faith, the substance of God walks with us, and that in itself is the spiritual death of ignorance.

I spoke about the shadow/shade that is the image or outline cast by you or others (a tainted shadow). Representing a self-led life or a life that causes others to throw their most poorly thought of image upon you, therefore damaging your thoughts of yourself or your character - if you or hearers believe them.

I spoke about the shadow/shade that is cast by a God himself or spoken of as a representation of a place for us to take refuge, or a covering, or represents a warning or indication of something to come, a present reality or a time-frame, or a sign from the Lord.

Psalm 91:1 AMP says *"He who dwells in the shelter of the Most High Will remain secure and rest in the shadow of the Almighty [whose power no enemy can withstand]."*

But we have a daily task to choose whether to be self-led or spirit led.

INTRO:

In 2 Timothy, Paul writes a letter to Timothy (his spiritual son) surrounding the theme of steadfastness in Christ while outlining affliction in Ministry, being active in the ministry, apostacy in the ministry (which is the turning away from God or abandoning one's faith after having professed it), and commitment in the ministry.

2nd Timothy is the last epistle or letter of Paul that he wrote from prison before his death. This was a personal letter from Paul to Timothy to express his concern that Timothy stays the course in the midst of many challenges he will face in ministry and to emphasize the importance of the Word of God. In chapter 1, he speaks of tears, testimony, and Desertion/Abandonment.

2 Timothy 1:1-7 AMP says...

"Paul, an apostle (special messenger, personally chosen representative) of Christ Jesus (the Messiah, the Anointed) by the will of God, according to the promise of life that is in Christ Jesus, 2 to Timothy, my beloved son: Grace, mercy, and peace [inner calm and spiritual well-being] from God the Father and Christ Jesus our Lord.

3 I thank God, whom I worship and serve with a clear conscience the way my forefathers did, as I constantly remember you in my prayers night and day, 4 and as I recall your tears, I long to see you so that I may be filled with joy. 5 I remember your sincere and unqualified faith [the surrendering of your entire self to God in Christ with confident trust in His power, wisdom and goodness, a faith] which first lived in [the heart of] your grandmother Lois and your mother Eunice, and I am confident that it is in you as well. 6 That is why I remind you to fan into flame the gracious gift of God, [that inner fire--the special endowment] which is in you through the laying on of my hands [with those of the elders at your ordination]. 7 For God did not give us a spirit of timidity or cowardice or fear, but [He has given us a spirit] of power and of love and of sound judgment and personal discipline [abilities that result in a calm, well-balanced mind and self-control]."

Timothy came from a religiously mixed household. His father was an unbelieving Greek, but his mother was Jewish. Both his mother and grandmother were believers of God. So, they taught him from a young child and he grew up learning the scripture.

Timothy was from the city of Lystra in Asia Minor [what is now known as the Asian portion of Turkey today], and was one of the places that Paul along with Barnabas and Mark visited to spread the gospel of Christ, during Paul's first evangelizing trip in 46-48 A.D. where he visited 6-7 cities/towns.

Quick note about A.D.

A.D. doesn't mean after the death of Christ, it is actually 'Anno Domini' in Latin which translates to "in the year of the Lord"; with 1 being year one of Christ's human life.

So Paul's first evangelizing trip was not 46-48 years after the death of Christ but actually 46-48 years from the year of Christ's birth. And since it is believed that Christ was roughly 30-33 years old when he died, Paul's first evangelizing trip was actually about 16 years after Christ died.

So you first have to subtract how old Christ was when he died, from the A.D. year, to get a real estimate of how long after Christ died, did these ventures occur.

Paul may not have necessarily met Timothy during his first journey in Lystra. But he would have definitely ministered to Timothy's mother and grandmother (Eunice and Lois) who were among the first converts from the Jewish community in Lystra, while Timothy was still a youth.

It was actually in the city of Lystra where the people thought that Paul and Barnabas were gods because they had healed a lame man who had been that way from birth and had never walked. But the man listened to them preach and by seeing that he had faith to be healed, Paul called out to him to 'stand up on his feet' and the man jumped up and began to walk.

This healing is what caused a ton of controversy, because some people believed God while others rebuked him and poisoned as many minds as they could. This eventually led to Paul and Barnabas being stoned and dragged outside of the city as if they were dead.

This was Lystra, Timothy's hometown, where Paul met Timothy.

We're first introduced to Timothy in the book of Acts. Timothy then joined Paul in his travels on his 2nd Missionary Journey, when Paul again passed through Lystra, but this time with Silas [because Barnabas and Mark had left Paul and went their separate ways, because of a disagreement about whether Jewish believers should eat with Gentiles].

Remember that Paul was a Jew called to minister the gospel to the gentiles. So because of that, there eventually began to be some Jewish customary and religious lines being crossed in order to minister effectively; and Barnabas and Mark, just was not willing to go down that road and continue to ruffle feathers. At least not at that time.

But this was the beginning of a father-son relationship bond between Paul and Timothy. This bond led to Timothy being regarded as Paul's most trusted friend and assistant. Consistently Paul gave him advice both personally and for the ministry.

One of the things I learned is that when Timothy was joining Paul, Timothy [who has a Jewish mother] was not circumcised according to Jewish custom as his father is Greek; and Greeks are gentiles. But one of the advantages of Paul, was that because he himself was a circumcised Jew, he was allowed to preach in the Jewish synagogues and enter the inner courts of the Temple in Jerusalem - but those privileges were only extended to Paul's Jewish companions. So Paul circumcised Timothy, as a Jewish believer in Jesus Christ, which served as a major benefit in their ministry as they walked together.

....

So fast forward, Paul is in prison and writing his final letters to Timothy leading up to his death.

I want to expound on some of the things that Paul charged Timothy with, while he outlines the items that Timothy is to be reminded of [so that he is prepared and not blind-sighted by the things that he will encounter in ministry]. Because after all, we are people!

MESSAGE:

1. Tears

In 2 Timothy 1, verse 4, Paul recalls seeing the tears of Timothy.

This more than likely must have referred to the time when Paul was arrested or when Timothy was left in Ephesus.

The scripture draws reference to the sincere, heartfelt, and even overwhelming emotions that can be felt (especially in farewells); and it highlights the trials and persecutions faced by the early Christians, while emphasizing the cost of discipleship.

Do you remember the feeling of an overwhelming sense of emotions, as those you knew and loved said farewell?

I'm not particularly talking about death, but the times when you knew that your time spent together as friends or as co-workers, or workers together in the ministry was coming to an end.

These are the times that you start remembering all the plans that you had in your mind, and all the things that you spoke of [that you hadn't yet gotten to do].

Did it leave you with feelings of discouragement and disappointment?

There are so many people that enjoy being alone and so many people who don't. Not that being alone is bad, but it should be looked at as a season and not your life's walk.

In all of God's creating, that he said was good; he said it was not good for man to be alone.

Paul doesn't only recall Timothy's overwhelming emotions but also Paul's desire for fellowship.

Fellowshipping is important.

It's companionship, being a part of a community and society. Ecclesiastes 4:9-10 NIV says *"Two are better than one, because they have a good return for their labor: If either of them falls down, one can help the other up. But pity anyone who falls and has no one to help them up."*

In 2 Timothy 1, verse 4, Paul also acknowledges that fellowship brings joy.

If you're constantly hanging around people and there is no joy, you're hanging with the wrong crowd.

If you're creating friendships and there is no joy, you're making the wrong connections.

If you're going to places and feel no sense of joy, you're going to the wrong places.

And if in everything you do, and everyone you meet, and everywhere you go, you come up empty every time, YOU are lacking the source of joy.

In the Greek, the noun joy translates to 'chara' meaning cheerfulness, calm delight, or gladness. The verb translates to 'chairo' meaning farewell, be glad, god speed, rejoice.

Is there a cheerfulness or a gladness that is linked to your character?

Do you bring that joy to the table when you fellowship, or do you seek to only absorb it from others?

It can be mentally draining for a cheerful person, if you are only seeking to draw from them - an exuberance that you desire to be around - but don't actually emit for yourself.

What does your farewell look like?

Are you clearly (outwardly expressing) a rejoice for others opportunities, even if it means that they will no longer be near.

Or, are you bitter and sour, giving off a spirit of guilt that the other person has to now decide what to do with.

Some people are not good at throwing things off of them. Some people hold on to things that slowly suck their joy right out from under them, until they don't even realize when they became this dull dry person.

When did you lose your ability to be overwhelmed with emotions?

To feel, to desire, to long for…

When did it become overshadowed by an unenthusiasm for life [where you naturally overlook others special moments, instead of celebrating with them]?

Is it because you've stricken the importance of it from your own life?

Disappointment is a natural feeling and momentary emotion. It prompts us to reflect on a momentary acknowledgement of nonfulfillment. But it is meant to prompt us to reassess our hope and expectations.

If we do not, we bring on the spirit of depression and hopelessness that is detrimental to our being [it cripples us and rob us of our future].

Lamentations in Hebrew is taken from the word 'How'. The title in the oldest known translation of the Hebrew Bible into Greek (the Greek Septuagint) means "Tears of Jeremiah". The book laments over the destruction of Jerusalem and the Temple of the Lord and concentrates on the past.

Yet in Lamentations 3:19-25 AMP there is a hope of relief in God's mercy, it says,

"Remember [O LORD] my affliction and my wandering, the wormwood and the gall (bitterness). 20 My soul continually remembers them And is bowed down within me. 21 But this I call to mind, Therefore I have hope. 22 It is because of the LORD'S loving kindnesses that we are not consumed, Because His [tender] compassions never fail. 23 They are new every morning; Great and beyond measure is Your faithfulness. 24 "The LORD is my portion and my inheritance," says my soul; "Therefore I have hope in Him and wait expectantly for Him." 25 The LORD is good to those who wait [confidently] for Him, To those who seek Him [on the authority of God's word]."

Even in a book that looks back in agony [at suffering] and laments, there is still a remembrance of hope that shifts the atmosphere.

It is a reminder of the sincere faith (that Paul talks about in 2 Timothy 1, verse 4) which lives in you. It is the type of faith that transcends generations [shaped by unique formative experiences, leading to new and fresh expectations and outlooks] because it fans into a flame, the gift of God that is evident in you through your anointing.

Remember that walking in your anointing is your investment in your overflow. And if you don't know what your anointing is, it's time to explore some options and start getting plugged in or saying yes to opportunities to serve.

If I give everyone a paintbrush, paint, and a canvas, and we were to paint a reflection of this message so far; everyone will have something different. The part that hits home to you will be reflected in your painting [depending on how well you were able to capture and express] through skill, what is illuminated to you.

And as everyone observes each other's paintings, the ones that causes everyone to stop, and look, and process what is conveyed before them [because it speaks to each one of us in a different way] means that we have just identified not just a skill, but a gift. **And if that gift positioned well [in a beneficial role] where God's presence and power is with them, it symbolically defines an anointing.**

This is what Paul is talking about that is symbolically represented in 2 Timothy 1, verse 6, by the laying on - of hands through the role of mentorship in spiritual growth.

Take the time to invest in the next generation of Christians.

Create workshops, show them the ropes, welcome new ideas, take to heart the importance of quality [not perfection but a spirit of excellence]. If something is wrong, fix it.

Take a class. Learn new skills. Even the older folks - you are not too old! Some colleges are offering continuing education classes, each season [some are free of charge to ages 65+] to learn and get certifications.

We have to volunteer, step up and learn what is needed to benefit the body of Christ, so that we can attend onto the issues; because it's seen and it's heard by others.

People are watching and it's not just visitors. It's not just members. It's the next generation!

They're looking at how you look or overlook.

Set good examples. Make reports on your progress. Be consistent. Don't fall back or sink into the shadow or take a back seat.

Come forward!

2 Timothy 1, verse 7 KJV says *"For God hath not given us the spirit of fear; but of power, and of love, and of a sound mind."*

If you're doing the right thing, there's no need to be ashamed. This is a part of our testimony.

2. Testimony

Let's look at 2 Timothy 1:8-14 AMP.

"So do not be ashamed to testify about our Lord or about me His prisoner, but with me take your share of suffering for the gospel [continue to preach regardless of the circumstances], in accordance with the power of God [for His power is invincible], 9 for He delivered us and saved us and called us with a holy calling [a calling that leads to a

consecrated life--a life set apart--a life of purpose], not because of our works [or because of any personal merit-- we could do nothing to earn this], but because of His own purpose and grace [His amazing, undeserved favor] which was granted to us in Christ Jesus before the world began [eternal ages ago], 10 but now [that extraordinary purpose and grace] has been fully disclosed and realized by us through the appearing of our Savior Christ Jesus who [through His incarnation and earthly ministry] abolished death [making it null and void] and brought life and immortality to light through the gospel, 11 for which I was appointed a preacher and an apostle and a teacher [of this good news regarding salvation]. 12This is why I suffer as I do. Still, I am not ashamed; for I know Him [and I am personally acquainted with Him] whom I have believed [with absolute trust and confidence in Him and in the truth of His deity], and I am persuaded [beyond any doubt] that He is able to guard that which I have entrusted to Him until that day [when I stand before Him]. 13 Keep and follow the pattern of sound teaching (doctrine) which you have heard from me, in the faith and love which are in Christ Jesus. 14 Guard [with greatest care] and keep unchanged, the treasure [that precious truth] which has been entrusted to you [that is, the good news about salvation through personal faith in Christ Jesus], through [the help of] the Holy Spirit who dwells in us."

Your testimony is more than the story of your test. It is the glory of the revelation of your experience. Let the Lord guide you into an effective testimony for the encouragement of the body of Christ.

It's good to tell your story and for us to track along with you [in expectation of what God is going to do]. But the bible says, **don't forget to come back and strengthen your brothers and sisters; and we do that with the glory of your victory.**

Sometimes we get so used to sharing the issues, but we shy away from sharing the victory because the enemy starts whispering things in our ears that – 'others going to ask you for something out of your blessings', or 'they're going to look at you differently', or 'they'll look to prey on your favor', or that 'they'd even start to treat you a certain way' [maybe singling you out]. So instead, you just come to church, and you sit down. No extra praise, no virtuous rejoicing; you're just calm, cool and collected. Is it because people can't know what God has done for you?

The bible encourages us, that we who have been rescued and saved should testify about it. A public declaration of gratitude and praise for the deliverance from trouble and our enemies. Psalm 107:2 KJV says *"Let the redeemed of the Lord say so, whom he hath redeemed from the hand of the enemy;'*

3. Desertion/Abandonment

Let's look at 2 Timothy 1:15-18 AMP.

"You are aware of the fact that all who are in [the province of] Asia turned away and deserted me, Phygelus and Hermogenes among them. 16 The Lord grant mercy to the family of Onesiphorus, because he often refreshed me and showed me kindness [comforting and reviving me like fresh

air] and he was not ashamed of my chains [for Christ's sake]; 17 but [instead] when he reached Rome, he eagerly searched for me and found me—18 the Lord grant to him that he may find mercy from the Lord on that [great] day. You know very well how many things he did for me and what a help he was at Ephesus [you know better than I can tell you]."

Even in the midst of hard times, the Lord will convict the heart of one [who doesn't let the talk of people or the fear of what it may cost them to be around you], hinder them from coming to help you in heighten times in your life (when everything is on public display).

In the midst of your dire situation, even as you pray or cry out to the Lord for yourself, don't forget to cover them also in prayer.

Some are going to help, and some are going to walk away. It is the plight of life. Hold fast to those who are with you and work together in peace and love, and let's not forget Joy. Because even God doesn't want to receive anything from you, if you're not cheerful. 2 Corinthians 9:7 ESV says *"God loves a cheerful giver."* Not someone who is reluctant or forced to do it. God isn't a drill sergeant; he has a heart and so does our brothers and sisters.

Paul formed a bond and connected with Phygellus and Hermogenes, but they walked away from him in his distress.

In the face of danger, what would you have done?

Would you put your safety and well-being ahead of the cause?

Would you leave the one in an attempt to save the others?

It doesn't mean that you've lost your faith, but it does mean that you have allowed your natural vision to dictate your perspective and direct your actions; verses letting your spiritual vision discern (and present to you) a spirit led plan for victory.

This aspect of desertion/abandonment comes around full circle with my first point 'tears' (the feeling of overwhelming emotions). One of the Greek definitions, references 'farewell' as the action verb of tears.

What do you do when others walk away from you?

We must come to a realization that some things are too much to bear for some people and learn how to release them.

Many people have reached pivotal life defining moments in life where people who were linked to them - just disappear.

It may be abrupt, or gradual, or may not even be done in the right way [based on one's maturity level or the circumstances], or maybe it occurred unintentionally through the course and flow of life.

Don't waste time, trying to figure it out. You have things to do; give people their space!

Maybe they have stepped into their own pivotal moments, or maybe there's a fear of this new season that you're stepping into; and they just can't. Or maybe, you've just reached a fork in the road, and the Lord is taking them down a different path.

There's so many possibilities, reasons, and so many excuses.

But meanwhile, God has placed so much in your hands. Do something with it!

Don't sit on ideas and things you've been charged with. Actually, try to count the unfinished tasks in your life and see if, even with all of the things that are undone, if you are still asking God for new direction and purpose.

Connect with others who can help; but don't forget to communicate with others, just for motivation and encouragement. Because even that is help!

Fear cripples the plan of God for your life, by whispering options to save yourself the trouble.

But it takes consistency to be purified and refined for good works, and to come out looking like pure gold.

In Closing,

When we fan the flames of our spiritual life, the temperature increases.

We'll have to understand that different people have different heat tolerances. And there will be an evident separation of metals from the gold.

There is a stress factor that will redefine us, to **S**tretch our capacity, cause us to **T**hink under pressure, exercise **R**estraint, teach **E**ndurance, **S**how us what we're capable of, and build our **S**trength.

I sometimes say, 'Blessed, but highly stressed!'

Our passion will become more fervent, and our willingness will materialize into tangible progress. And those who are standing in the balance, will have to learn how to let their yes be yes and there no be no. Meaning, if they say yes, there should be action, commitment, and effort. But if they say no, they shouldn't stand in the way and become a stumbling block to those who are answering the call.

As we grow in the spirit, it is our pursuit to maintain a mature palate for digestion, while wrapped in a childhood vitality, a renewed vision, and revived drive for the Kingdom of God [that sees hope in everything, sees beauty in the rubble, can run and not be weary, and carry love, kindness and joy - like a treasure chest that's full of gold and all their most precious things].

People who know how to separate the positive from the negative (when it is fully charged).

In Matthew 18:3 KJV Jesus said *"...Verily I say unto you, Except ye be converted, and become as little children, ye shall not enter into the kingdom of heaven."*

All of this takes purposeful consistency to fan the flames.

2 Timothy 1:6 "This is why I remind you to fan into flames the spiritual gift God gave you."

AMEN.

Chapter 3 - Author's remarks

This sermon contains so much gems for the body of Christ.

I was truly in awe at what the Lord was saying, because it is so true. Light bulbs were going off all over the place!

God's word brought such a needed resolve to things that we all struggle with in the Church community, in our workplaces, our families, as well as our social lives.

From emotions to our personal stories, to staying the course, I really saw how consistency played a vital role in our overall stability.

One of the biggest ah ha moments for me was the unfolding and revealing of the gap between a skill, a gift and an anointing. You may naturally possess a talent or be well advanced in a particular learned skill, but when your talent/skill can cause others to see themselves [reflecting on the purpose, dreams, visions, plans, and promises of God] it becomes a gift to the body of Christ. And when that Gift is positioned well and backed by good leadership and the power of the Holy Spirit (mentorship and spiritual growth) it becomes your anointing. Dwelling in that level means that we can now inhabit in the fullness of the overflow [the abundant life God has for us]. This is where our cup overflows; but consistency determines if we remain there.

May God continue to bless you and bring to life, words that will motivate you to live in the fullness of his plans for you.

The Cost of the Sword

Chapter 4

The Cost of the Sword

RECAP:

In the first message I spoke about prayer and how our surrender is vital in receiving our daily bread.

Our prayers literally ask for favor, blessings, healing or some form or portion of abundant life that can only happen if the Lord's will is done on earth, as it is in heaven. But that requires us to live in the Kingdom [meaning be in the world, but not of it]. And we do that through faith that fuels our anointing.

As a child in the kingdom of God, being anointed is your portion; but without faith you are stifling your investment to your overflow. Your anointing is your investment in your overflow.

The process of faith is more than confidence, it is actually the evidence of revelation, illumination, and an understanding, that directs us daily through the Word of God, into the things that are to come. This is our daily bread.

It is the Lord's response to our communication and interaction with him, that translates [from our natural breath and movement] into a spiritual conversation, that then returns to us in a physical manifestation [confirming that words are not void].

Isaiah 55:11 NKJV "So shall My word be that goes forth from My mouth; It shall not return to Me void, But it shall accomplish what I please, And it shall prosper in the thing for which I sent it."

In my second message I spoke about how contentment is not comfortability.

It is easier to get off of a couch than it is to get off of a bean bag; and easier to get off of a chair than it is to get off of a couch. **If we position ourselves in the appropriate seat for our season, our response will be a bit smoother as we shift into the next season or assignment.** If you're too comfortable to move when prompted, you become a liability to yourself; because your motion is out of alignment with the will of God.

Living a self-guided life is a liability because you are moving in your own time, and your own pace, and based on your own feelings, and your own calculations, and based on where you want to go. Our **own** decisions does not take into account all the unseen and unknown things that won't work out for our good.

Romans 8:28 NKJV says, *"And we know that all things work together for good to those who love God, to those who are the called according to His purpose."*

I spoke of a redefining of stress. That it **S**tretches your capacity, causes you to **T**hink under pressure, exercise **R**estraint; it teaches **E**ndurance, it **S**hows you what you're capable of, and it builds your **S**trength.

Stress is only a significant contributor to many health problems, because we have not been properly trained to identify and use it correctly, therefore it destroys us.

I went on to speak about the shadow and the substance.

When something gets in the way of the sun, it makes a shadow.

Our shadow reveals perspective, which engages our humanity to walk by sight. But the substance of God puts to death spiritual ignorance by a renewal of our mind that changes our point of view by introducing discernment, to guide our emotions in preparation for what is seen and unseen.

It presents choices before us to preset a particular spiritual attitude, that paves the way to allow us to hear what the Lord is saying through spiritual guidance so that we walk by faith.

Psalm 23:4 NKJV says *"Yea, though I walk through the valley of the shadow of death, I will fear no evil; For You are with me; Your rod and Your staff, they comfort me."*

Meaning, even though we are walking through life with a predisposed shadow of Self [which engages our self-seeking and self-advocating humanity to walk according to our own point of view]; through faith, the substance of God walks with us [introducing discernment that changes our perspective].

This gives us spiritual guidance to approach life's experiences; so that at times when we react to the momentary emotion of fear, we can be comforted by a Shepherd who walks with us [chastising the spirit of fear] so that even though evil lurks, it does not hinder your path.

Things that are evil, come with a spirit of fear. Not a momentary emotion, but a spirit of fear that seeks to attach itself to you. This ensures that even though you may not experience certain things in life, that you are traumatized, just by the very knowledge of it.

I spoke about the shadow/shade that is the image or outline cast by you or others (a tainted shadow). Representing a self-led life or a life that causes others to throw their most poorly thought of image upon you, therefore damaging your thoughts of yourself or your character (if you or the hearers believe them).

This tainted shadow originates from our predisposed nature to always intercept and interfere with what God is doing.

Disobedience falls within this shadow. Believing others negative reports over God's definitive statement, falls within this shadow.

Joshua 5:6 NIV says *"The Israelites had moved about in the wilderness forty years until all the men who were of military age when they left Egypt had died, since they had not obeyed the Lord. For the Lord had sworn to them that they would not see the land he had solemnly promised their ancestors to give us, a land flowing with milk and honey."*

I spoke about the shadow/shade that is cast by God himself or spoken of as a representation.

This shadow originates from the substance of God, that leads us (through spiritual guidance) to walk by faith.

Many times that means that the children have to trek through the wilderness too [because they belong to the house, and they live in the house; and babes in Christ have to be raised in the house]. So, it left the new generation at a disadvantage [in a place where they had to grow up in homes, where irrational ideas, bad behaviors/habits, ill mentalities, emotional baggage, strife, and trauma] that should have been cut off along the way [through discipline, devotion, and good leadership], still lingered among them.

Joshua 5:7-9 NIV says *"So he raised up their sons in their place, and these were the ones Joshua circumcised. They were still uncircumcised because they had not been circumcised on the way. 8 And after the whole nation had been circumcised, they remained where they were in camp until they were healed. 9 Then the Lord said to Joshua, "Today I have rolled away the reproach of Egypt from you." So the place has been called Gilgal to this day."*

Circumcision was a sign by God of a covenant (a seal of the righteousness which was in Abraham by faith).

Romans 4:11 says that *"He received the sign of circumcision, a seal or confirmation of the righteousness which he had by faith while [he was still] uncircumcised—this was so that he would be the [spiritual] father of all who believe without being circumcised—so that righteousness would be credited to them,"*.

At Gilgal, Joshua renewed the covenant through this act of purification of the new generation.

This covenant represents the shadow of God of a place for us to take refuge, or a covering, or represents a warning or indication of something to come, a present reality or a time-frame, or a sign from the Lord.

Psalm 91:1 AMP says *"He who dwells in the shelter of the Most High Will remain secure and rest in the shadow of the Almighty [whose power no enemy can withstand]."*

But we have a daily task to choose whether to be self-led or spirit led.

In my third message I spoke on the topic that consistency fans the flame.

2 Timothy was a personal letter from Paul to Timothy to express his concern, that Timothy stays the course (in the midst of many challenges he will face in ministry), and to emphasize the importance of the Word of God.

In chapter 1, he speaks of tears, testimony and desertion/abandonment.

I spoke of how Timothy's tears and desire for fellowship resonated with Paul (his spiritual father).

Do you know that when you come and go, (as quietly as you do), that you are not remembered?

Your presence is not vivid enough to be recalled into memory as a significant moment. But did you know that when you are overwhelmed with emotions or inhabiting in the light and the joy of fellowship, that it actually leaves and imprint on the heart of the Lord? An imprint that is so significant that you are remembered night and day, just like Paul felt.

Your sincere faith is what causes the Lord to move within you, because your fleshy (spiritual) heart feels something.

Remember that he replaced our heart of stone with a heart of flesh, so that he can search through the intricacies of the depths of our thoughts, feelings, and perceptions (the ideas and predictions we come up with, about our lives and where we see things in the near and further future).

The Lord searches our hearts for the things that create memories or triggers that stings us, or shuts us in like a clam. The things that's left bruises and scars that no one knows about. The things that causes us to be full of fear and hyper reactive to every movement in the world around us, or less reactive to the possibility of danger [not necessarily unaware of imminent danger], making some people the ultimate explorers.

The Lord searches out the things that make us innocently naïve on one hand, and full of knowledge and wisdom on the other hand. He searches out why we respond the way we do, or the things that cause us to go through life just skating across the surface.

Now, it's possible that some people missed that heart surgery from a heart of stone to a heart of flesh 😊. But for those of us who have it. Your heart responds to his presence, because his presence is significant to you. Because if it's not, you simply won't respond.

This is what defines your faith, shaping your experiences, leading to new and fresh expectations and outlooks because it fans into a flame the Gift of God; that if positioned well with wisdom, mentorship and spiritual growth, and backed by the Lord's presence and power, defines your anointing. I'll say that again…

This (your sincere heart that responds to his presence) is what defines your faith, shaping your experiences [through new visual lenses], leading to new and fresh expectations and outlooks [where discernment precedes perspective] because it fans into a flame the Gift of God that he reveals to you [just because you said yes]. And if this Gift of God is positioned well with wisdom, mentorship and spiritual growth, and it is backed by the Lord's presence and power [the unquenched expression of the Holy Spirit], it defines your anointing.

This is what Paul is referencing as he encourages Timothy to walk in his anointing, in 2 Timothy 1:6 AMP, he says *"That is why I remind you to fan into flame the gracious gift of God, [that inner fire--the special endowment] which is in you through the laying on of my hands [with those of the elders at your ordination]".*

I spoke about testimony [not being ashamed or refusing to testify of the Lord's goodness but strengthening our brothers and sisters with the glory of your victory]. Testimonies are not just stories, it is a personal account of God's grace and mercy.

I also spoke about disappointment, abandonment, and farewells. Where does that leave you?

Even in the midst of whatever is going on in your lives, is there a remembrance of hope that is powerful enough to shift the atmosphere.

Hope that reminds you that you still have Joy. That there's still work to do and new connections to be made.

When we fan the flames of our spiritual life, the temperature is going to increase; and different people have different heat tolerances.

There's an evident separation when we go through the refining process (like gold); and consistency is how we going to stay the course [despite the stress factor].

INTRO:

1 Samuel takes us from the birth of Samuel [who became not only a prophet but was the last of the Judges of Israel] to the death of Saul [who was the first of the Kings].

In between Samuel grew up in the temple.

His calling sent him directly to individuals who God called, appointed, anointed, instructed, and even those whom God expected more from as leaders. To those people, he gave explanations, warnings, and decrees from the Lord.

In those days, if Samuel showed up at your door, you should feel a little intimidated.

According to 1 Samuel 8, technically there were 2 more judges over Israel [under Samuel]. They were his 2 sons [who kind of reminded me about Eli's situation].

1 Samuel 8:1-9 NKJV, says…

"Now it came to pass when Samuel was old that he made his sons judges over Israel. 2 The name of his firstborn was Joel, and the name of his second, Abijah; they were judges in Beersheba. 3 But his sons did not walk in his ways; they turned aside after dishonest gain, took bribes, and perverted justice. 4 Then all the elders of Israel gathered together and came to Samuel at Ramah, 5 and said to him, "Look, you are old, and your sons do not walk in your ways. Now make us a king to judge us like all the nations." 6 But the thing displeased Samuel when they said, "Give us a king to judge us." So Samuel prayed to the Lord. 7 And the Lord said to Samuel, "Heed the voice of the people in all that they say to you; for they have not rejected you, but they have rejected Me, that I should not reign over them. 8

According to all the works which they have done since the day that I brought them up out of Egypt, even to this day—with which they have forsaken Me and served other gods—so they are doing to you also. 9 Now therefore, heed their voice. However, you shall solemnly forewarn them, and show them the behavior of the king who will reign over them."

Samuel appoints Saul as King because God agreed to the demands of the people, that were based on the wrong motives.

Not only wrong motives but it was the wrong choice because, Saul was from the tribe of Benjamin, and in Genesis 49 Jacob makes a decree to all his sons (who are the 12 tribes of Israel) of what will happen to them and their descendants in the future.

In Genesis 49:10 AMP to Judah he says this *"The scepter [of royalty] shall not depart from Judah, Nor the ruler's staff from between his feet, Until Shiloh [the Messiah, the Peaceful One] comes, And to Him shall be the obedience of the peoples."*

So, we know the choice of Saul was of God's permissive will.

Permissive will is the idea is that even though this, allowing of your free will decisions, is not what God has specifically planned for your life, that he can still work through the situation to accomplish his will.

It's the loooong way around. Where you basically have to suffer the consequences of your decisions and actions, until you eventually get to where God wants you to be.

Every time God gives you direction and you say: "but God?" and he says, "fine do it your way!" He is basically reluctantly agreeing to your wilderness season; because you've just placed your own stretched shadow, right before his promise of milk and honey for you.

So all this came to pass and Samuel later anoints David (a shepherd boy) to be Saul's successor, after Saul's disobedience to God.

Most know the well-known story…

David encounters Goliath on the battlefield and wins and quickly gains a high rank in the army. David forms a brotherly covenantal bond with Jonathan (Saul's son), but Saul develops a hatred for David and places him in battles (dangling the prize of marrying one of Saul's daughters as a trap for David) while he was really hoping that David would be killed in battle by the enemy. David excelled at the test, which was a big win for Israel and in *1 Samuel 18:28-29 NKJV "Saul saw that the Lord was with David and that his daughter Michal loved David. 29 So he grew even more afraid of David, and he was David's enemy all his life."*

After that, David spends practically a decade living on the run from Saul. Even after Saul's death, David still did not quickly become King, because Saul's household fought to keep the kingship within the family. So, there was war between the house of Saul and the house of David.

MESSAGE:

The book of Samuel covers a period of about 115 years. Chapter 21 is surrounding David in his plight of fleeing death at the hand of Saul.

In 1 Samuel 21, Nob was the officially the first place that David went after fleeing Saul's kingdom for good and saying goodbye to Jonathan. He went to Ahimelech the priest and basically lied to him, telling him that he was on a secret business for King Saul, and that he needed food, and a weapon because this secret mission was urgent. When the reality was that he fled the kingdom with nothing, and he needed some form of physical sustenance and protection.

But Doeg the Edomite, who was in charge of Saul's servants saw David when he went to Ahimelech the priest and knew that the priest gave David provisions and a sword. But not just any sword. 1 Samuel 21:9 NKJV says *"So the priest said, "The sword of Goliath the Philistine, whom you killed in the Valley of Elah, there it is, wrapped in a cloth behind the ephod. If you will take that, take it. For there is no other except that one here." And David said, "There is none like it; give it to me."*

The sword was a part of the spoils of victory and represented both a significant military and a spiritual trophy [a reminder of God's deliverance of Israel, through David's faith].

It was a military custom to dedicate captured trophies in sacred spaces reflecting gratitude and devotion to God. So Goliath's sword came under the care of Ahimelech, the priest at Nob. And there it was wrapped in a cloth behind the ephod, which is the priests sacred apron that is worn during religious ceremonies.

So, this sword was constantly revealed and seen by the priest, every time he picked up his garment to perform a ceremony. And even though he didn't know the real reason or truth behind David's visit to the temple, the connection between David and Goliath's sword was not a memory that the priest had to dig deep to find. Ahimelech the priest, made a direct statement of reflection to David and his victory, and offered it to him, almost as if it was preserved for David for this very moment. And David, confirming that there is none like it, made no hesitation to take it.

Now how big was this sword? Goliath himself was a big guy [the bible says that Goliath was 6 cubits and a span, which is about 9 feet 9 inches tall – about the regular height from the floor to ceiling of most homes or apartments]. Maybe you pictured that he was much bigger - but when stories are told over and over, our imagination tends to soar. So, it is understandable how David in his youth was able to pick up Goliath's sword to behead him, after he hit Goliath in the head with the stone and he fell face down on the ground. Goliath's sword may have just been about twice the size of the typical army sword.

I want to talk a little about the sword and what it represents.

The bible often talks about God's word as the Sword of the spirit. Eph 6:17

Hebrews 4:12 talks about the sword being living and active and also sharper than any two-edged [natural] sword, as it has the ability to pierce into the division of soul and spirit to discern the thoughts and intentions of the heart.

I've watched a sword being made or forged, and it starts with a plan [an image/design that a bladesmith creates to guide them in the process of the creation]. It includes the very intention for making the sword, how sharp it will be and the function of it.

The bladesmith either pours molten metal into a steel casting, or take a piece of iron or steel [sometimes layers of iron] and heat it up at really high temperatures in a forge (a type of hearth used for heating metals).

They heat the material to just over 2000 degrees until it turns yellow.

When something is yellow hot, it doesn't just melt skin, it turns bones into ashes. Then, they have to shape it by hammering both sides into its desired shape as they go back and forth from the forge, reheating it as needed.

When the shape is established, it has to be reheated to normalize the steel [to refine the structure and relieve internal stresses, caused by the hammering]. This reheat has to bring the blade up to a non-magnetic temperature of just over 1400 degrees, repeating the process making sure that all the red color [that was caused by the heated friction of the hammering process] has left the steel. This improves toughness and ensures that the edges are firm.

It then takes sanding and grinding, again reheating and dipping in oil [quenching the steel to strengthen it].

One of the most important factors is transferring the blade from the fire to the quenching as quickly as possible [because if you are too slow, the blade won't harden properly], then slowly reheat it to relax the brittleness and stress induced by the quenching process. Then begins the process of creating the handle.

In Matthew 10:34 AMP Jesus tells his disciples *"Do not think that I have come to bring peace on the earth; I have not come to bring peace, but a sword [of division between belief and unbelief]."*

Can you imagine that this process of creating the blade is the process of going from a place of faithless belief to the place of faith-full belief?

What are you made of and how do you withstand the heat [when you're being hammered and grinded and sanded and then experience a little relief in the quenching process, only to but put back into the flame again]?

But you don't stay there!

Some of our most crucial seasons are inaccurately labeled as mistakes because the temperature is so high that even those who come near begin to sweat, and they wonder what you've done to get to this place.

They don't understand that you're being forged. Even you yourself sometimes don't understand that you're being forged.

The process is so rapid and abrupt from the fire to the quenching, back to the fire and again to the quenching to lower heat. You don't even understand the God is ensuring you don't crack under the pressure [that creates the aspect of stress that he is ironing out]. The stress that stretches you, that causes you to think on your feet, the restraint that you won't fall or be tempted so easily because you know how to exercise self-control, the endurance that you will be consistent and stay the course. He's showing you what you're capable of so that he can build your strength [so that when he's ready to use you, you can slice through any situation without succumbing to crippling emotional thoughts that you yourself have the ability to create].

You'll be able to stand and guide and lead without cowering; and give an answer of wisdom without any prior knowledge on the subject. You'll be able to rightly divide the word of truth.

But what if you're in the forging process for too long and instead of strengthening, you're thinning out and weakening.

It's an indication that you are not conforming to the master's will. So, you're going back and forth and back and forth (heat, hammer, heat, hammer, quench, heat, hammer, heat hammer, quench). You keep going back to the hammer.

Every time he tries to bevel an edge you resist to be molded, so instead of becoming a choice weapon in the hand of God you become something unfit to be used.

The thing is, as Christians we're always being forged. But there's seasons for the forging process. As we enter into new levels, we need to be forged for those levels.

To the world, Jesus came to bring salvation and peace. But to his disciples he came to bring a sword. A sword that is effective in any season.

When people give excuses about understanding the word or the bible, it is an indication that they are still in the salvation process (the process of being saved); not the discipleship process where God is forging swords. Be vigilant, but be understanding, and patient.

These swords that the Lord is forging is not something that we are acquiring through our faith walk, it is something that we are becoming. Our lives become a representation of a blade, where God holds the handle. Not for the slaying of others in their sin or because of their sin, but to represent a process of sanctification that is attained through spiritual growth and transformation.

Sanctification is a state of separation unto God, or being set apart for his special use and purpose. It is the putting off of one's old self and the putting on of a new self (one filled by the spirit).

In Closing,

Sanctification has easily become the enemy of the world because no one desires to be tried and tested. The enemy is after believers, not to kill them, but to steal, kill and destroy the Gift of God, your prayers, your anointing, the overflow of abundant life, and the ultimate goal of eternal life.

And people are running from the catastrophe and the fear, or just walking in their own shadows (being self-led, self-made, and ultimately self-destructive).

But many are not running into the house of the Lord.

The enemy does his best work by devaluing the cost of the sword [sanctification], making it seem like it's a bad trade off against the cost of living your life. He does this while inflating his agenda as something that is cheaply attained; while hiding and covering up the true cost of one's soul [that many don't know of until it's too late].

Ephesians 6:14-20 NKJV says *"Stand therefore, having girded your waist with truth, having put on the breastplate of righteousness, 15 and having shod your feet with the preparation of the gospel of peace; 16 above all, taking the shield of faith with which you will be able to quench all the fiery darts of the wicked one. 17 And take the helmet of salvation, and the sword of the Spirit, which is the word of God; 18 praying always with all prayer and supplication in the Spirit, being watchful to this end with all perseverance and supplication for all the saints— 19 and for me, that utterance may be given to me, that I may open my mouth boldly to make known the mystery of the gospel, 20 for which I am an ambassador in chains; that in it I may speak boldly, as I ought to speak."*

We have an opportunity to be equipped to go into the world and not be overcome by it.

We have doctors, lawyers, teachers, administrators, and many professions where we encounter people that are looking and seeking for something they don't know of.

They're looking for answers and something that can satisfy. And the gift of God within you lifts up a standard and it is seen through the way you live your life, how you respond to others, how you present yourself, and what you have to say.

It can either lead others to life in Christ or do absolutely nothing about their wide path to destruction.

Today through the scripture 1 Samuel 21:9 the High priest [the Lord] is saying that the sword (which is the word and the enemy of unbelief), whom you acquired through the putting off of your old self, is here. It is wrapped in the cloth of sanctification and is behind the ephod of good leadership [that is prominently displayed in the house of the Lord]. If you will take that, take it. For in this house of the Lord, there is no other weapon, except that one here. And David said, *"There is none like it; give it to me."*

AMEN.

Chapter 4 - Author's remarks

There is a saying that 'you catch more bees with honey' but guess what? The bears also come too. The full story of David shows us several points:

1. That you can be chosen, anointed and elevated; and you can do everything right and want the best for everyone, but you still need to be vigilant of the bears.
2. There's going to be times when God reveals others evil plans towards you, but your closest companions may not want to believe it [because they just can't see or accept what you have experienced in private] until it's too late.
3. Staying the course means that you're going to have to run alone sometimes, but there are always safe-spaces designed to remind you of who you are, and to provide you with resources and sustenance to stay motivated and keep you moving.
4. Opportunities for retaliation will present themselves, but it will only be a test of your character, do not allow your emotions to precede your discernment.
5. Because the dust has settled and you've taken your position, it does not mean that you've arrived (to sit down and relax). The real work does not end at good leadership but rather it begins the process of training up future generations to not depart from it.

Many look at those who seem to present themselves as the ultimate believer as the extreme side of Christianity. The tightly pressed lips and laser eyed Christians who appear to have an agenda of striking fear into the hearts of others as a hook designed to win souls for the Lord. Those who scorn what you touch, look down at what you say, and are super selective of who they share their space with. These are the shoes that many don't want to follow.

But these seemingly 'untouchable people' in the house of the Lord have caused many stumbling blocks in the paths of those whose abundant life rests and depends on them getting to the place of sanctification.

If sanctification continues to be viewed as a level where people lose control of their lives, and trade it in for a life that they have absolutely no desire for, then they will always live with one foot in the church and one foot in the world [for fear of losing out of the one life they have to live].

Sanctification is really a model of a victorious life. A life filled with the fruits of the spirit that [because of one's heart to serve] has revealed gifts that symbolize a life filled with purpose and freedom. A life that demonstrates that you are competent, accountable, empathetic, relatable, transparent, vulnerable, and genuine. A life that others are proud to call both a leader and a friend. Sanctification defines your ability to not only teach but the fact that you are teachable (rooted in humility, openness and willingness).

Sanctification highlights the fact that you are different, set apart, and someone worth protecting and holding fast to.

Sanctification means that you are a sword with a double edge, that is fit for good use (prepared, reliable and efficient) and held by the master's hand [a hand that is wrapped around your life, providing blessings, favor, abundance and overflow.

This Changes Everything!

Chapter 5

This Changes Everything

RECAP:

This message is the last in a series of messages that touched on many concepts, including:

Prayer, your daily bread, the process of faith, anointing, overflow, comfortability vs contentment, self-guided life vs purpose-driven life, walking by sight vs. walking by faith, a redefining of stress, perspective, discernment, spiritual ignorance, fear, images of ourselves, covering, spiritual guidance, staying the course, fellowship, testimony, overwhelming emotions, vivid presence, joy, a heart of flesh, the Gift of God, spiritual growth, mentorship, farewells and disappointments, hope, refining, consistency, wrong motives, permissive will, provision, protection, victory, the intentions of the heart, internal stresses, structure, friction, toughness, strength, peace, belief and unbelief, faithless and faithful, pressure, temptation, self-control, endurance, crippling emotional thoughts, conforming, resistance, choice weapon or unfit item, molded, effective, salvation, disciples, not acquiring - but becoming, sanctification, being set apart, transformation, tried, tested, the ultimate goal of eternal life or ultimately self-destructive, inflating, true cost of one's soul, equipped, lifting up a standard, responding to others, presenting yourself, what you have to say, how you live your life, a life in Christ or path to destruction, putting off of your old self and good leadership.

When you look at these many words, just being honest, how many of them cause you to remember pivotal moments in your life?

What does your walk look like? It's great to have a personal relationship with the Lord, but does it benefit anyone other than yourself?

Does it benefit your family, your friends, your neighbors, acquaintances, even strangers? Does it benefit the church, and the kingdom of God?

Maybe it just benefits some of those groups, but not all of them.

INTRO:

1 Corinthians is one of the early books of the New Testament that provides insight into the worldly and struggling church, specifically at Corinth.

Back then there was about a half a million people in Corinth which is located in Greece. It was a very commercialized city that was big on materialism, immorality, pleasure, and sensuality. The city went through vast periods of political influences that increased its territories making it dominant in trade, land and sea traffic. They facilitated the transit of ships and cargoes and built major roadways and highways and several harbors that allowed travelers huge time-saving shortcuts on their many voyages, rather than taking the long way around. Like many nations, they rose and fell and rose again.

In the New Testament, Corinth had been reestablished by Julius Caesar and became the administrative capital of the Roman province of Achaea (Achaia) in Europe, an important center of commerce. It was a basic hub for communications, banking, trade, and buying and selling on a large scale. It held many athletic contests, similar to those in Olympia [where the Olympics derived from]. It was known as an international city with a mixed population, and these Corinthians are who Paul wrote several letters to.

These were Christians that were primarily poor and many of the people coming into the church came from paganistic practices [meaning either they didn't believe in religion at all or they worshiped false gods usually by default of their local area tradition].

Corinth was one of the original cities that never slept. Always busy. Much like New York.

Now why is it that many church folks are still poor and not rich?

For one, there is a rich mentality and there is a poor mentality.

The rich mindset places great importance on learning from their mistakes, whereas the poor mindset always makes moves with the intention that there are always options to be bailed out of their mistakes.

One lives in both the present and the future [by making decisions that will benefit them later on in life], while one lives in constant fear of missing out or trying to pacify emotions or keep up a state of appearance.

There are many resources available that lay out the differences between these two mindsets. They reference key opposing components like:

- spending vs investing

- blaming vs taking responsibility
- just getting by vs learning to succeed
- focusing on what was lost vs what can be gained
- patterning life based on work earnings vs taking full inventory of the total value of all that have been accumulated
- contentment with life as it is vs a drive that life has a lot more to offer
- being reluctant to change vs taking opportunities necessary to impact both growth and goals
- looking down on others vs celebrating others wins and encouraging
- procrastinating vs maximizing your time, moments and experiences
- giving up or doing nothing vs addressing the issues

In the popular book 'Rich Dad Poor Dad', Robert T. Kiyosaki teaches on personal finance, which among other things, debunks the notion that you need to make a lot of money to become rich. He shows charts that depict the typical cash flow patterns between a poor, middle class, and rich person:

- A poor person's money flows from their salary and out through their expenses (such as taxes, rent, food, transportation, and clothes). They have no liabilities or assets. It's what many would call a 'hand-to-mouth' lifestyle.
- A middle-class person's money also flows from their salary and out through their expenses, but in addition to the poor person's expenses, middle-class person's have liabilities (such as a mortgage for a

home, car loans, credit card debt, and school loans) of which the payments are also included in their overall expenses. They usually have very little to no income producing assets.
- A rich person's money flows from their assets (such as real estate, stocks, bonds, notes, and intellectual property) into their income (which includes earnings such as rental income, dividends, interest, and royalties).

Robert explains that while everyone has expenses for the cost of living, the cash flow is what tells the story of how each person handles their money. And although our lives are affected based on our income and expenses, our financial position (balance sheet: assets and liabilities) is really what operates our financial performance.

He talks about the reality that if your income matches your expenses, then you simply don't have enough money to invest in assets. But if we focus on growing our assets and minimizing our liabilities, we can truly tip the scale of our financial performance (profit and loss: income vs expenses).

Robert basically puts into perspective how the rich get richer [when assets generate more than enough income to cover expenses and the balance gets reinvested back into assets, which continue to grow and subsequently increases income with it].

So how do we change our mentality so that we can live in the abundance that God has for us?

It begins with an inward spiritual shift that causes us to trust, yield, and respond to the Holy Spirit and sound leadership, leaning not on our own understanding.

Many Christians today are trying to live a settled lifestyle [fixed in our ways and our space and our routine], while everything around us fluctuates. The only difference between us and Abraham, Moses, Job, Jacob, and Joshua, and many other prominent chosen ones in the bible is that they were living a nomadic lifestyle [always positioned to move when the Lord spoke, no matter how much they had grown in size].

How can you say you're willing to attain the promises of life, if you are not yielding to physically go where he needs you to go?

We are worried about distance, cost, how we are going to be sustained, how things will be different, and how the people are different.

But all these things were not revealed to those men of the bible, when the Lord said to leave the place where they were.

I'm recalling that Jacob ended up being led to a place where his son Joseph was gone. And years later while still saddened by his loss, he had to endure a famine [that usually leads to death]. But he humbled himself and did as the Lord guided him and sent his sons into Egypt to ask for food. This led to the discovery that his son Joseph was not only alive but positioned in a place for his family's very survival and increase.

Jacob was reunited with his lost son and made a move that would change history forever. There he and his family thrived, living their best lives. But when there is a poor mentality of comfortability, you just live for today. There is no thought of ownership or generational wealth. And when you become too big for your own good and don't have your own, others start to view you as a threat. But instead of running you out of the land or destroying you, they subject you. And this is what happened to the children of Israel.

The issue of oppression by the enemy really tends to be a crippling result of poor mentality.

So how does God take you to a promise of ownership (the promise land) from the issue of oppression by the enemy?

He is really trying to take us from a process of salvation [being delivered from our old selves, our old ways, and our old mentality], and into a place of sanctification [where we are set apart and can live in the perfect will of God].

MESSAGE – Part I

Many of the stories in the Old Testament are showing us what the men and women of God had to go through, in the process of being delivered (salvation).

And how even though he set apart leaders [that he raised up through sanctification], the people themselves never actually got to that stage in their faith walk.

Do you think that when God went silent for 400 years [in the period between the Old and New Testaments], that it was because he just got tired of the people going through the fire, but never actually becoming a sword?

How long does he have to fight for us, before he can fight through us?

40 years in the wilderness may kill out 1 generation and save one, but 400 years kills out 19 generations and saves 1. It means if you only had one child, and that child didn't have any children; after 19 generations have passed, your line doesn't even become a thought in history.

The difference between Salvation and Sanctification is that with salvation, there's so much work to be done in our lives [because we've acquired so much junk and made so much of a mess of our situations], instead of being in a place where we are working on our advancement, increase and overflow [through God's will and purpose].

I'm not just talking about physical junk, but also mental junk and spiritual junk.

We become hoarders of a world that has captured the 3 major areas of our lives (our body, our mind, and our spirit).

When this happens, we can no longer see things as a child would. And when our father (God) speaks to us, many times we can't budge. We say things like, 'this is just who we are!' But it's because we become so set in our ways and as stiff as a trunk.

'In order to move a tree with a hardened trunk, it needs to be cut down.' And that's just the harsh reality.

The bible says, what is it worth to gain the whole world and lose your soul. The whole world is not all the riches that exists, it is simply filling [to your own hearts content], the pleasures of the body, the knowledge of the mind, and the freeness of your spirit [that generally keeps you from being in a place of complete surrender to God].

So, we're going to have to position ourselves to where the issues of life doesn't look like our old self anymore, but looks more like…

- Having a hard time figuring out which class to take vs. which bill to pay.

- Who we can bless vs wondering who's in the place to bless us.

- How can we help vs. what's in it for us

----

1 Corinthians deals with Sanctification, whereas Romans deals with Justification.

Justification is the starting line. It's basically the initiation of the process of Salvation.

It is the act of being declared righteous/not guilty because of the acknowledgement that Jesus Christ has finished the work required on the cross [paying the penalty for our sin], offering to us His free gift of life.

This was basically what I spoke about in 'The Shadow and the Substance'. Where we acknowledge there is an interception of light that is cast by our own self-image. But there is also shadow that originates from the substance of God that cancels out everything that would have otherwise deemed us unworthy and guilty of our

sin. It is the acknowledgement, declaration and acquittal from sin.

Now, like the sinner on the cross next to Jesus - he basically obtained his free gift of life [in that instant through justification], and then he died.

Now in a situation like that, justification is all you need to obtain the free gift of life, if you then die shortly afterwards [and God will be the judge of that].

But for those of us who keep on living, Justification is not enough. It's kind of like having an intention to take an ice bath, because you heard that it's good for you, but after dipping your toe you renig [and you go on your merry way living life as usual].

That's justification by itself. It didn't initiate salvation, you just acknowledged it, you declared it. And if that is your only step - you moved on. As some people say, 'I tried it, it wasn't for me.'

So, whenever you hear preachers talking about being justified, it's a call for new converts to enter into the process of salvation. But for those of you who were justified years ago, when you first met the Lord, it's not enough. For you, much is required.

The problem is many of us don't know how to cheer each other on.

We know it's hard, we know it's a shock, but we stand and watch silently and hope and pray that they'll jump in anyway and receive the benefits of being a follower of Christ. But it doesn't work that way. So, we have to cheer each other on, and be each other's biggest supporters.

One of my sister's is a teacher and this is something she says all the time, and it's true.

Now, Salvation is where the rubber meets the road!

Salvation is the process of being saved. It is the spiritual and eternal deliverance granted by God to those who accept His conditions of repentance and faith in the Lord Jesus Christ, in whom alone it is to be obtained, upon confession of him as Lord.

So, through us receiving Christ as our Lord and savior we move to the state of living by Grace. This is basically what I spoke about in 'Consistency fans the flame'. Where we **believe, convert, and follow**.

We talked about Lystra, where Timothy came from and how - him, his mother and grandmother believed in the Gospel of Christ, and because of that, became new converts and followed in the Gospel. This is the process of staying the course of faith through the Word of God. Despite affliction and many people going in different directions, commitment is necessary to win this race called life. Because your soul, can't afford this kind of loss.

Sanctification [even though the word sounds so spiritual] is simply walking in alignment with the will of God. This is basically what I spoke about in 'The Cost of the Sword'

Have you ever had people tell you, 'there's something special about you!' It's not something to use as a cue to melt away into your feelings [and cause you to regard that person as something more in your life than they are actually qualified to be], but rather something that should make you aware of the confirmation that you are reflecting the light of a substance that's far greater than you can ever imagine.

It is a prompt in life that you should not take what is in you for granted. And to be aware that the enemy lurking around looking for an opportunity [through the observance of flattery remarks] to see how you respond.

While everyone is looking for a chance to get to know you better, Satan is looking for opportunities to put stumbling blocks in your way [to try to slow you down or stop you from getting to your destination]. And that destination is Sanctification.

For instance, when you drive your tire runs over many things. Your tire can handle so much pressure and rugged terrain, but the small pointy nail is what would stop you in your tracks. **It's interesting to know that something so small can affect one of the most important components required to take you to your next destination.**

The small pin hole is the thing that the enemy would use to slowly seep the life from within you. Till you wonder how you could become such a fearful person.

You would come to realize in life that as you grow in faith, the things that you are fearful of will automatically minimize.

So, if you are growing more and more afraid, it is an indication that you need to be filled with the spirit of God; not only the word. Because sometimes we read the word and are well versed in it, but we are lacking his presence (the spirit) that creates a fullness.

The bible says in John 6:63 KJV that *"It is the spirit that quickeneth; the flesh profiteth nothing: the words that I speak unto you, they are spirit, and they are life."*

John 1:4 KJV says *"In him was life; and the life was the light of men."*

These scriptures substantiate what Isaiah 41:10 AMP says *"Do not fear [anything], for I am with you; Do not be afraid, for I am your God. I will strengthen you, be assured I will help you; I will certainly take hold of you with My righteous right hand [a hand of justice, of power, of victory, of salvation]."*

Then 2 Timothy 1:7 says KJV *"For God hath not given us the spirit of fear; but of power, and of love, and of a sound mind."*, the AMP puts it this way *"For God did not give us a spirit of timidity or cowardice or fear, but [He has given us a spirit] of power and of love and of sound judgment and personal discipline [abilities that result in a calm, well-balanced mind and self-control]."*

In 1 Corinthians Paul stressed that our problems should be solved by spiritual principles not psychological expedients. Meaning, when it comes to carnalities in the Church [such as things that cause division, disorder, and difficulties] Paul stresses that we don't solve these problems by thinking of convenient methods that are advantageous to us [because many of those options are not really morally good or acceptable].

For example, we can make the statement that it might be expedient not to pay the worker until he finishes the work. That is a plan that conveniently works for us. But it can be unfair to the worker, who then has to come out of his own resources based on good faith that when the work is done, he will be reimbursed.

We go to restaurants, we eat and when the bill comes we then pay. And some people, if they are not satisfied or something is wrong with their meal they use the bill as an opportunity to bargain with the workers on why they should not be charged for something, or why they should get a discount.

This kind of expedient psychology is how most of the world operates, but it is the opposite of how God works.

This is where the scripture 1 Corinthians 10:23-24 AMP comes in, that says *"All things are lawful [that is, morally legitimate, permissible], but not all things are beneficial or advantageous. All things are lawful, but not all things are constructive [to character] and edifying [to spiritual life]. Let no one seek [only] his own good, but [also] that of the other person."*

What if Jesus said, 'I'm not going to die for your sins until you are sanctified, and then you would earn the right to have Grace (so that your life would not be lost)'.

Then who would get to heaven?

Instead, he sets spiritual principles for us using his life to demonstrate the very aspect of Grace. These principles show us that nothing we do can earn our way to receiving Grace. He paid the price, and you received the gift.

You didn't die in that car accident because of the Grace of God. You didn't suffer severe consequences of high levels or inconsistencies in your body (like others have) because of his Grace.

There's a cost that's going to come before we get to reap the benefits. But whose going to pay for it?

Some may say they had to fight like hell, but are you willing to fight like heaven?

MESSAGE – Part II

When the ark of the Covenant was captured by the Philistines, it brought many plagues and misfortune to them. Eventually when they had enough, they gave it back. But it stayed at the house of Abinadab the priest for about 20 years [when Israel repented] and then for about another 40 years [during the time that Saul was King], until David finally became King and went to retrieve the Ark.

Abinadab's son's Uzzah and Ahio drove the new cart that carried the Ark. The bible says in 2 Samuel 6:6-8 NKJV, *"And when they came to Nachon's threshing floor, Uzzah put out his hand to the ark of God and took hold of it, for the oxen stumbled. 7 Then the anger of the Lord was aroused against Uzzah, and God struck him there for his error; and he died there by the ark of God. 8 And David became angry because of the Lord's outbreak against Uzzah; and he called the name of the place Perez Uzzah to this day."* Perez Uzzah means Outburst against Uzzah.

The threshing floor was a flat and open area used for separating the grain from the chaff. It symbolized a place of judgement and decision. Threshing floors were usually located in a place with strong and steady winds. Hilltops were traditional locations.

Now why would David bring the Ark of the covenant to a threshing floor where farmers process the grain of their crops?

I found out that in ancient days, it wasn't only used for agricultural purposes, but also as neutral places of gathering, places of political treaty, mourning, sacrifice and as building sites. In fact, because these areas were unique and valuable it meant that the owner could benefit by charging for use.

Sadly Hosea 9:1 NLT also attributes usage of the threshing floor as unfaithful acts against God. It says *"O people of Israel, do not rejoice as other nations do. For you have been unfaithful to your God, hiring yourselves out like prostitutes, worshiping other gods on every threshing floor."*

Now the Ark of the Covenant was the earthly throne of God. It was to be carried exclusively by the Levites, and it's handling was governed by strict divine instructions to be carried on their shoulders by its poles.

Not on a cart.

So here, the priests sons are carrying the Ark of the Covenant on a new cart that they made for it and it's being pulled by oxen. And the ox stumbled and Uzzah held it [I guess to steady it], and he instantly died.

I have three questions?

1. **Shouldn't the priest have known better?**

    But then I thought,

    The Ark, was not kept in a temple for about 3 generations.

    This reminds me of people whose church is solely in their homes. It gets to a point where you become complacent about the divine instructions that God has given us for the benefit of the body of Christ. You forget the importance of fellowship [not forsaking the assembling of ourselves together, exhorting one another, exercising the gifts of the spirit, the encouragement of the people with testimonies and singing, and breaking bread together].

2. **Why was the ark brought to the Nachon's threshing floor?**

   Nachon was a Benjamite. Remember that Saul was the wrong choice because he was from the tribe of Benjamin. So here we go again with another bad choice [bringing God's most holy presence here on earth to a place that is not only out of alignment with his word, but also a place that is a reminder to God of the unfaithfulness of his people towards him].

   In Genesis 49:27 NKJV Jacob makes this decree to the tribe of Benjamin, *"Benjamin is a ravenous wolf; In the morning he shall devour the prey, And at night he shall divide the spoil."*

   Wow! For a father to say that about their child, their temperament must be pretty unapologetically intense. Looking to capitalize on any opportunity that benefits themselves [no matter who sees or who gets caught in the crossfire], but then secretly sharing the benefits with those who can't be seen associating with them in the light. 'Personal gain, at the expense of others.'

3. **Why did the ox stumble on what was a wide-open flat area?**

   Deuteronomy 25:4 NKJV says *"You shall not muzzle an ox while it treads out the grain."* The ox was typically used as a valuable asset for plowing and threshing. So, it is not muzzled to be allowed to eat (while working) to ensure it was well fed and able to effectively perform its duties. But because it was harnessed together with a yoke it is possible that being at the threshing floor would have caused it to automatically attempt to do something it is prone to doing while being on the threshing floor, which is bend down to eat; which could have caused it to stumble [along with the strong winds], because the ox was restricted.

Bringing the Arc of the Covenant back was like a reward to King David, who desperately wanted to do the right thing in the eyes of the Lord and the people.

I could imagine that taking the Ark to the threshing floor was a way to put the Ark on display [as a grand announcement before entering Jerusalem].

But after 3 generations of the Arc not being moved:

- The priests became complacent and forgot what needed to be done.
- The King made a bad decision, taking the ark to Nacon's threshing floor.
- The ox mis-stepped/stumbled in a place known for judgement and decisions.
- And Uzzah touched what he shouldn't have touched, costing him his life.

But instead of humbling himself, David was angry that Uzzah died.

Have you ever been angry at your situation?

You had good intentions, but it all went up in smoke?

And instead of making it right, you decided not to deal with it at all.

David decided to leave the ark for 3 months with Obed-Edom the Gittite, from the priestly tribe of Levi, until he came to an understanding on how God wanted him to do things; and then he went back to get the ark [this time doing things the right way].

2 Samuel 6:12-15 NKJV says *"Now it was told King David, saying, "The Lord has blessed the house of Obed-Edom and all that belongs to him, because of the ark of God." So David went and brought up the ark of God from the house of Obed-Edom to the City of David with gladness. 13 And so it was, when those bearing the ark of the Lord had gone six paces, that he sacrificed oxen and fatted sheep. 14 Then David danced before the Lord with all his might; and David was wearing a linen ephod. 15 So David and all the house of Israel brought up the ark of the Lord with shouting and with the sound of the trumpet."*

There's a cost that's going to come before we get to reap the benefits.

And when you come into an understanding and right standing with God, are you going to go back for the Ark?

Are you willing to sacrifice, toxic ways and unbeneficial habits and a poor mentality to signify that you are serious about walking into your blessing and your overflow?

This is a personal assignment.

Because we can't be an effective member of the body of Christ, emanating joy as we fellowship, and getting behind good leadership as a unified people, edifying the body of Christ, if we don't make good personal choices.

David took a step back gathered himself, educated himself; he put on his ephod [clothed in the word of God]. For God did not give him a spirit of fear, but of power and love and a sound mind. He went back, and he tried it again [doing things the right way, according to the direction of the Lord].

In Closing,,

The church at Corinth (the city that never sleeps), was termed a Church full of charismatic gifts [including tongues and prophecies], but also a church that was not free from Greek pride [characterized by immaturity, immorality, and disunity]. And we still see this in churches today.

Many of these issues are consistent problems because people seek their own good and not for that of the other person.

They become complacent of what they see as always being there. And when the time comes to make the move, they forget to reverence it as something that is sacred.

They become rogue, not seeing value in community. And so, the domino effect continues.

What's going to change all of that is a desire and a maturity to step into Sanctification.

Are you ready to take hold of the promises of God?

Justification is like a mother knowing that she's about to go into labor. **Salvation** is going to the hospital and the process of having the baby. And **Sanctification** is taking that baby home in 3 days and knowing that everything you do counts towards the growth and advancement of life.

Stepping into sanctification is your place of abundance. That is where the good stuff happens. All of your growth and advancement in life. Your anointing and your appointing. Your stepping into your purpose to be driven into your overflow.

You don't need your sail boat anymore [that used to fight against the direction of the winds] because now you're in a ship sailing in deep seas, cutting through the winds.

Your character is being fortified for an edifying spiritual life. One that isn't marred by a poverty mentality but mature enough to understand that **money is a resource and not the source of eternal life.** It's not something to be loved, and idolized, and not something that you will allow to cost you your soul.

But money is something that is going to advance the kingdom of God. A poverty mentality is not just about money. It's about our ability to break free from spiritual ignorance and live in the power, love, sound judgment, and personal discipline that result in a calm, well-balanced mind and self-control (2 Tim. 1:7 AMP).

This is where our lives begin to shape up and look like a glistening sword, and not just an inflamed piece of metal.

And with God's guidance [holding the handle on that blade] we are not going to fail. We are going to be victorious every time. And we are going to teach others how to follow in that victory and not just keep it to ourselves.

AMEN.

That is why I remind you to fan into flame the gracious gift of God, [that inner fire--the special endowment] which is in you through the laying on of my hands [with those of the elders at your ordination]. 7For God did not give us a spirit of timidity or cowardice or fear, but [He has given us a spirit] of power and of love and of sound judgment and personal discipline [abilities that result in a calm, well-balanced mind and self-control].

2 Timothy 1:6-7 AMP

A Message from Bishop Elect – Pastor Martin C. Scott

Dear Reader,

This book not only teaches us to walk in our anointing but also how we can preserve or maintain the anointing in the over-flow.

The anointing is a gift that is given to believers in Christ, engineered and supported by the Holy Spirit (Eph 4:8).

Every good thing we receive from God is handed over to the holy spirit who distributes it (to several) as he wills. So it is He (holy spirit) that acts as the distributor of the fathers gift to his children.

The over flow is a bonus or extra privilege given to us so that we can operate more effectively and efficiently in the kingdom.

Anointing maintenance
(Maintaining the overflow)

A. Knowledge

It is said "what you don't know can hurt you."

Having a knowledge of God's promises is in his will concerning you. It puts you in an advantageous position, allowing you to make the necessary adjustments to set your house in order to receive the anointing that breaks yokes and destroys burdens.

B. Understanding
Prov 4:7

It's important for every child of God to possess the spirit of understanding [after you have heard and received the vision for your life, family, business or church, or maybe a personal matter].

The next step is to understand the directive or what needs to be put in place to accomplish the task.

Habakkuk 2 - Teaches us to make the vision plain; for he who understands it will allow the operation of the Holy Spirit to accomplish his will, so that we can be partners and beneficiaries of the overflow.

Understanding is the conduit for the overflow to keep flowing because understanding establishes the overflow.

C. Wisdom

Many Christians today, live underprivileged lives (not enjoying the full benefit of the overflow), only because there is a lack of wisdom. Prov 4:7

Wisdom creates a friendly environment for the anointing to flow.

In many religious and social establishments, people are not living up to their full potential; and it's sad because the father wants us to prosper. He wants us to prosper even as our sole prospereth, but it will take wisdom in the overflow to accomplish the task.
Many times in building families, cooperations, business, churches, and even our personal lives [because of lack of wisdom] we allow structure to override creativity. When we allow this, we give no room for growth thus we forfeit the overflow.

In a world of political, social physical and spiritual decay, what every child of God needs to do is seek knowledge, understanding and wisdom so that we can live and operate through and by the Holy Spirit. This combined with the overflow will allow us to combat and to stay focused until the coming of our Lord.

Prov. 4:2-9 gives us a sample of living in wisdom accompanied or enhanced by the anointing in the overflow.

1. "Forsake her not, and she shall preserve thee…"
2. "Love her, and she shall keep thee."
3. "Exalt her, and she shall promote thee."
4. She shall bring you honor
5. She shall give you grace
6. She will give you a crown of glory.

My prayer is that this book will be used as a tool to draw you closer to the presence of the Holy Spirit and the overflow that is so needed in our lives today.

Bishop-Elect Martin C. Scott
Hebron Evangelical Fellowship Ministries

Who is Glenesha McIntosh?

> A Servant
>
> A Wife
>
> A Mother
>
> A Teacher
>
> A Dreamer
>
> An Author

I came to know Glenesha over 30 years ago. I saw her grow from a seed of righteousness into a tree that is planted, bringing forth fruits in this season.

She has not only inspired me but has been an inspiration to Hebron and the world by extension. With many more land to possess, I extend to Glenesha my blessings in her life long journey of service in God's kingdom, knowing that 'A giver is never a loser' (Ecc. 11:1).

As you read this book, my prayer is that the wisdom and knowledge of God will become fertile in your life.

"Jesus doeth all things well".

Bishop-Elect Martin C. Scott

Who is Glenesha McIntosh?

I have known Glenesha McIntosh for over 15 years, as a member of Hebron. I was also one of her instructors in the General Bible class at the Hebron Evangelical Bible Institute.

She was a very enthusiastic student; eager to learn about the 'Word' and always prompt to accomplish a task within or ahead of the deadline. Because of her diligence and her dedication in her studies she continued on to the Advanced Theology class where she graduated as Valedictorian in the class of 2015.

Today, I can say that Glenesha is truly an anointed orator of God's Word.

She is able to break down her message into 'bite size' pieces, as she shares biblical insight [combining both the spiritual and physical aspect as well as a clear picture of God's plan, purpose and instructions] so that mankind can navigate life.

This book is a spiritual makeover which I'd recommend as a must read!

Min. Lydia Philip

"The Spirit of the Lord GOD is upon me, Because the LORD has anointed and commissioned me To bring good news to the humble and afflicted; He has sent me to bind up [the wounds of] the brokenhearted, To proclaim release [from confinement and condemnation] to the [physical and spiritual] captives And freedom to prisoners, 2 To proclaim the favorable year of the LORD."

Isaiah 61:1-2 AMP

"Jesus read the scroll of the prophet Isaiah …

Luke 4:18-19 AMP

"THE SPIRIT OF THE LORD IS UPON ME (the Messiah), BECAUSE HE HAS ANOINTED ME TO PREACH THE GOOD NEWS TO THE POOR. HE HAS SENT ME TO ANNOUNCE RELEASE (pardon, forgiveness) TO THE CAPTIVES, AND RECOVERY OF SIGHT TO THE BLIND, TO SET FREE THOSE WHO ARE OPPRESSED (downtrodden, bruised, crushed by tragedy), 19 TO PROCLAIM THE FAVORABLE YEAR OF THE LORD [the day when salvation and the favor of God abound greatly]."

Unless otherwise noted, all scripture is taken from the King James Version (KJV) of the Bible (Public Domain in the USA).

Scripture quotations & marked bible versions of KJV, NIV, ESV, NKJV, AMP, and NLT taken from:
- King James Bible. (Public Domain in the USA)
- Holy Bible, New International Version®, NIV® Copyright © 1973, 1978, 1984, 2011 by Biblica, Inc.® Used by permission. All rights reserved worldwide.
- The ESV® Bible (The Holy Bible, English Standard Version®) copyright © 2001 by Crossway Bibles, a publishing ministry of Good News Publishers.
- The Holy Bible, New King James Version, Copyright © 1982 Thomas Nelson. All rights reserved.
- Amplified Bible Copyright © 2015 by The Lockman Foundation. All rights reserved www.lockman.org
- Holy Bible, New Living Translation, copyright © 1996, 2004, 2015 by Tyndale House Foundation. Used by permission of Tyndale House Publishers, Inc., Carol Stream, Illinois 60188. All rights reserved.
- NIV & KJV Side-by-Side Bible
Published by Zondervan www.zondervan.com

Nelson's Compact Series – The New Strong's Compact Bible Concordance – James Strong, LL.D., S.T.D.
Copyright © 2004 by Thomas Nelson Publishers

A Popular Survey of the Old Testament by Norman L. Geisler © 1977 by Baker Academic a division of Baker Publishing Group

A Popular Survey of the New Testament by Norman L. Geisler Copyright © 2007 by Norman L. Geisler

Published by Baker Books a division of Baker Publishing Group

Vine's Complete Expository Dictionary of Old and New Testament Words with Topical Index – Keyed to Strong's Reference Numbers – by W.E. Vine, Merrill F. Unger, William White, JR.
© 1984, 1996, Thomas Nelson, Inc., Nashville, TN;

Rich Dad Poor Dad by Robert T. Kiyosaki
Copyright © 2012 by Robert T. Kiyosaki
Published by Plata Publishing, LLC
Word Search, Synonyms, and Definitions taken from:
- https://www.google.com/search?
- https://www.thesaurus.com/browse/ ©2019 Dictionary.com, LLC
- Merriam-Webster Online (www.Merriam-Webster.com)
- Merriam-Webster Online Dictionary copyright © 2015 by Merriam-Webster, Incorporated
- Merriam-Webster Online Thesaurus copyright © 2015 by Merriam-Webster, Incorporated

Britannica – sluicing
https://www.britannica.com/technology/sluicing

Guide To Sword Making: Learn How To Forge A Sword. By Kristin Arzt
https://www.thecrucible.org/guides/bladesmithing/sword-making/

Britannica – Corinth
Article was most recently revised and updated by Michele Metych.
https://www.britannica.com/place/Corinth-Greece

World History Encyclopedia - Threshing Floors of the Bible by Patrick Scott Smith, M. A. published on 27 July 2022
https://www.worldhistory.org/article/2050/threshing-floors-of-the-bible/

How Long Was the Ark of the Covenant at Abinadab's House?
by Paul Schlehlein
https://betweentwocultures.com/2014/12/25/how-long-was-the-ark-of-the-covenant-at-abinadabs-house/

www.ingramcontent.com/pod-product-compliance
Lightning Source LLC
Chambersburg PA
CBHW050650160426
43194CB00010B/1878